Vrasidas Karalis

FAREWELL TO ROBERT

GW00536275

Vrasidas Karalis

Farewell to Robert

Brandl & Schlesinger

First published by Brandl & Schlesinger in 2023
www.brandl.com.au

Cover and book design by Andras Berkes-Brandl

ISBN 978-0-6454998-6-5 print

A catalogue record for this book is available from
the National Library of Australia.

Printed in Australia by Ligare

Robert Joseph Meader
(17 January 1958 – 10 May 2022)

My love,

I didn't expect you to leave me so suddenly. You were unwell for the last five years, but you always managed to get out of trouble. In 2020, your leukemia mutated; yet doctors stressed that Hodgkin lymphoma has a high survival rate. "He will live through it," they said, "with the new treatments." But you didn't. You left suddenly and that suddenly makes your departure cruel and disorienting. I still try to make sense of how and why. I blame the doctors, I blame the system, I blame myself; yet it is irrevocable, unrelenting, and futile. You are not here anymore to keep everything together. And I, who has explored the mysteries of presence, must now come up with images, consolations and fancy words for your absence. Suddenly, meaninglessness bursts out of everything. What happens when death is not a metaphor anymore? When it transforms our world into shadows. I have lost all sense of material gravity since you left: I speak from the realm of monochrome abstractions. And what truth exists in them?

The house we bought is a hole into nothingness, our garden a jungle without footpaths, your paintings on the walls, windows to an abyss. Our home is a living testimony to the absence of your hands. I never understood how you managed to keep it so clean, so tidy. Even when you were unwell, your hands knew how to place every-thing in their natural position. "Where does this live?" you used to say. Clothes in the wardrobe. Dishes in the cupboard. Cleaning products in the laundry. Simple and uncomplicated, our home looked like a beautiful picture, something out of the Victorian illustrated books you used to love so much. And it was a revelation to me, the chaotic Mediterranean.

Now that you are gone, the slow march of indifference and resignation takes over the space you cared so much for and struggled to keep transparent. Dust and fluff and dirt, which I see time and again and care not to remove. I am afraid that anything I do could erase your presence from the world of our beloved things and objects. I can still see your fingerprints on the silver and the crystal. The teddy bear of your childhood looks at me in confusion and bewilderment. Your toothbrush, your Miyake perfume, your green Oroton umbrella, your school bag, all make indecipherable noises. Your wooden Steiner toys look like mystifying messages left behind by aliens. Your briefcase, your scarf, your watch, your brush, your notebooks, your shoes, mementos of thirty years together – they all talk and talk about somebody missing. They keep calling out your name. The neighbors say, "We haven't seen Robert for some time. Where has he gone?" "He has moved on," I reply without looking at them. "He has gone elsewhere."

Last night, our two dogs, Maisie and Milo, small and discreet, were cowering inside your night gown, your sleepers, and trousers. We adopted them in early February to help with your recovery process. They were five weeks old when you brought them to our home. Yesterday, they were sniffing frantically on the couch where you usually sit to watch television. Every time I tried to move them, they started barking. Months later, and your scent is still everywhere. Yesterday, they rushed through the garage and hid under your car; they yelped and lamented, scratched the door, and sobbed. Now you have become an atmosphere and a mood, and I am surrounded by you without you being here. I look after our home, yet I am not in there anymore, although I still am.

Early January 2022. Our last month of tranquility and balance. We were sitting in our roof garden looking at the sunset and the bleeding clouds of the western horizons. "I love this time of the year," you said. "It reminds me of my childhood in Woy Woy. Kookaburras, currawongs, lorikeets, magpies, parrots. Each one of them with their distinct melody." Now, sitting in the same spot, I hear your words as sibylline oracles. The sun is going down. The depthless horizon is in flames. Birds are flying around. Trees are shaken by cold winds. I immerse myself into the moment and struggle not to bite my lips. You have moved on. You are elsewhere. Yet you are here. You have left all these birds behind.

For the first few months of the year, your health was fairly stable. You did go to hospital twice, but you came out almost invigorated. You attended auctions and purchased exotic hats from the fifties. You bought paintings and artwork. You ordered vintage clothes from Florida. Marimekko fabrics from Finland. Italian glass bottles from New York made in the sixties. You immersed yourself in a flurry of activity. Less than seventy days later all changed. One night you collapsed at home, and I called for an ambulance. It arrived three hours later to take you to the Royal Prince Alfred Hospital. You stayed there for two weeks. "Mild pneumonia," they said. When you were discharged, your health seemed stable again.

Then, you had the third Covid vaccine, which sent you into several days of total lethargy. In April, they had booked you in for a minor operation to insert a portcatch under your skin for easier chemotherapy. They gave you anesthesia. I told them to keep you in the hospital for the night. They declined. You came home, went to bed and, as you got up, you fell on the ground and had a horrible seizure. I called for an ambulance. 22 April, 2022. I still remember how you looked back towards our apartment when they took you away. It was a farewell, a painful good-bye: "Look after Vras," said your affectionate gaze to the things we loved. I was left abandoned in our house. A great silence followed. The home was not our home anymore.

You stayed there for ten days. One day they called me after I had just left your room. "Come back," they said. "He is having sepsis. His blood pressure is extremely low. He has no time left." I rushed back to you. You were in bed laughing and joking when I arrived. "I am fine," you said. "I will get out of it again." They transferred you to Wolper Care Hospice for recovery. "He will stay there for two weeks and then he will come back home. We can restart chemotherapy again in one month," the doctors said. Monday, 2 May, 2022. I believed them. "He needs time to recover, with good food, attention and rest", they insisted. The food was terrible and there could be no rest in that place. People were dying around you every day. I should have known better.

Then, within a handful of days, everything unraveled. That Friday at the hospice, we were planning to visit the house of the Durrells in

Corfu; or take the ferry from Piraeus to Naxos. You were lucid and talkative. On Saturday, you asked me to let you sleep early. You felt tired, you said. On Sunday, you were silent. You looked at me with resignation and despair. On Monday you fell into a coma. I was standing next to you mute and terrified. You breathed heavily and painfully. I smiled when you looked at me. "Stay with me," were the last words you said. I had no intention of leaving. But I was under the delusion that you would get through it. "We have been here before," I said. I slept next to you those last three nights. On Tuesday, May the 10th at 10.15 in the morning, you left quietly, without a sigh, or gasp or even a whimper. You turned to the left and stopped breathing. I had just gone out to wash myself. Your cousins Suzan and Deborah were in the room. You simply turned to the left and you were gone, gently as you had lived, noiselessly as you had always behaved. The moment of death didn't change you. You didn't slip into panic. Serenity everywhere. Grace in all.

The deafening silence was interrupted by someone crying out loudly, "Agape mou, kardia mou, agape mou". You lay lifeless and redeemed, while I was snatched by the vertigo of grief and inconsolability. The disease had destroyed your musical existence, your hands were turned inwards, your eyes had almost disappeared, your mouth hung wide open. I kept your body close to mine, trying to keep you warm, and touched your sweet beard. "My love, my heart, my love," I kept crying out. In an archetypal gesture of prehistoric lament, I kept your head on my chest, looking upwards into the depthless abyss of the hospital ceiling, re-enacting the mother of all mothers crying for her son. The nurses removed me from the room in haste. "You must get out," they insisted. I was in no state to resist. Then you were taken away and I stood at the door looking at the bed, which was empty, like the tomb in Jerusalem.

Standing in the enormous, icy, abysmal corridor of the choleric hospital, I looked around but there was no exit. I felt dizzy, taken over by a strange whirlwind. My stomach was retching, a buzzing took over my ears, my hands spasmed in a way I had never experienced before. I felt like a stunned animal, suddenly bereft of all senses. I thought that I could sense shadowy movements of invisible entities everywhere. You were one of them, hovering all over the place, but my eyes were full of tears and could not see you clearly in that immense throng of souls. "My love, my heart, my love," I kept repeating. Then I lost all sense of time and found myself being taken by a friend back home in utter despair, with the sun mocking me remorselessly.

You looked bigger in death. Solid, homeric and immaterial. As paleness took over your face, lips and skin, your body exuded an agonizing serenity. Nothing around you seemed to move. There was an absolute stillness, as if all movement converged on your inanimate body. Everything was turned inwards, imperceptibly; objects, humans, animals all became suddenly omens, symbols of our ancient days and bygone actions. Humans, animals, machines could be barely heard, the urban frenzy, speechless, preverbal, a sonic continuum of senselessness without the humming and the screeching of vital excess.

The undertakers transferred you to the morgue in Newtown, so close to our home. I had passed by that place so many times. I never paid any attention. And suddenly I had to go in there and sign documents, exchange polite words and give permissions. The next day Deborah and Suzan came to our home and took the clothes they would put on you in the coffin. I was frozen. You were still in the hospital linen, naked and covered with a white sheet. The undertakers gave me the clothes. "Can I put his socks on?" I dared ask. "Yes, yes, go on," they said. But as I approached, I hit my head against an unseen wall and could only hear people rasping. From that dark place, they sat me on a chair, and I could see them dressing you, and then taking you away. "What am I doing now?" I asked myself. "Where am I?" And then I started repeating, "Where am I? Who am I? Robert, turn on the light… I see nothing."

❧

Tuesday, May 10th, 2022. The moment when all our world collapsed, when its center was swept away. I look around and reality is in visible flux, things become watery, melt, disperse, yet time thickens and congeals, as my body moves through it like being stuck in gluey mud. I am talking nonsense, I know. You are not here. How can I define myself through past tense? Can we grasp what is gone when the victorious now forces us to keep moving?

"Are you responsible for his grave?" the undertaker asked. "It's a tad expensive these days but there are many options and price ranges. Will he be buried in Sydney or elsewhere? Sydney prices are exorbitant. Fifteen to twenty thousand for a plot. Also, his tombstone will take time to be installed," the young clerk continued mechanically, "as there are marble shortages in our imports from China." Looking at his watch, he added: "What price range are we talking about?" He gave me some papers to sign. Everything had disintegrated as in a broken mosaic, with its colored pebbles scattered everywhere. And I kept answering his questions without knowing what I was talking about. "I must go," he said eventually. "I have some other commitments."

For five minutes, I was left alone in the big cold room, knowing that you were lying locked in a metallic fridge a few inches away. We were separated by a wall. I put my hand on its surface, just in case everything was a terrible mistake, a bad dream perhaps, but, no, nothing. I knocked at the cold wall, whispered your name, but no response. A nice lady came in, shook my hand and gave me her condolences. "I am Greek too," she said and guided me out to King Street, which was instantly transformed into a demonic and absurd place. Your death changed the benign experience of our beloved street into a pandemonium of terrifying creatures. We had walked this street side by side, so many times. Now it was cold, alienating, infernal. I repeated a French word, tristesse, I said to myself, tristesse. Thanatos is tristesse. I don't understand why.

∽

My excessive reaction, I know, is rather embarrassing. From the beginning of our common life, you showed me the truth of "less is more", something that I can never forget. You showed me the truth of endurance, forbearance, of carrying on, the deep values of your Australian Englishness. Fairness was your scripture. "I cannot do such a thing," you used to say. "It is unfair, inhuman, cruel." And you were talking about euthanizing your aged cat, or cutting down a tree, or criticizing a colleague at school. You were shy and unostentatious. You never forgot your year-twelve teacher at Northmead

High School, Ms. Reynolds, who at the end of the year, made her assessment: "Robert is a true Stoic." All your life you thought that she meant that you were a loser. But you were more than a Stoic – and she meant something completely different.

I don't watch the news on television or read newspapers anymore. Some echoes from the outside world break through the walls of our ransacked Troy, incoherent sentences, indecipherable puzzles. Your presence linked them all together, gave them order and scope, established a pattern of recognition through their unnecessary complexities. You avoided the noise inhabiting the mental slumber imposed by trivialities. Your absence now dissolves the unconscious and meaningful attraction of events; everything is a strange and relentless flow of representations without a connecting thread. There is nothing to guide my mind through the labyrinth of disparate episodes. Your gaze is gone, and hours have become long seasons, immeasurable by watches and clocks or other human devices.

I struggle to retrieve your voice; its tone, pitch, tempo, separate it from the echoes of the other beloved dead that inhabit my mind. Brother, father, mother, Tony, Alkis, your mother, your sister, your father. We have been surrounded by death over the last ten years. In our personal underworld, the voices of the dead gradually become indistinguishable; deep in our despair they force us to give them back blood and memories, to recall them back to bodily existence. My purpose, for there is no other purpose anymore, is to deliver your existence to the sanctuary of language, erect your monument against futility.

Yet, the thresholds of the mind are crossed and suddenly life regains its pristine and brutal originality. Sunsets are dreary now; every evening, flying bats hover over our garden. Birds, airplanes, objects of all shapes become traces of departing deities. For the last six weeks it has been raining endlessly. Fog and humidity descended after you left; as if we had come from movies, scenes from mystical forests and Scandinavian sagas, us the children of luminous motherlands.

The day of your death was sunny and warm. Later that night, it started raining again. I watched the movement of the water on the windows, and my mind went to our first nights in this new house, the enthusiasm, the optimism, the euphoria. Finally, aged sixty, we had bought our first home. That was your great achievement, truly it belonged to you. From our home to your grave, the journey was fast and horrible. I thought that I was dreaming when they were burying you. I had a momentary disturbance of thinking. I saw your body dressed in the clothes you wore for concerts as it was lowered down into the deep earth: velvet jacket, blue tie, white shirt, your woolen cardigan, your Scottish trousers, Athenian socks and Italian shoes. Now I remember each one of them; where you bought them, how much you paid, when you used them, the occasions, the people you met. Old images spring out of the still lakes of oblivion, they have always been here, lurking in the shadows ready to infect us with their tearful epiphanies.

I open my eyes and suddenly I find myself at the church preparing the details of your funeral service. The priest asks which Christian devotions I would like to put on the coffin. "A crucifix, and the Bible", I respond automatically, "and Cardinal Newman's *The Dream of Gerontius*". You loved Elgar's music on the poem. I found our small rare 1912 edition and put on your casket amongst the roses. Now from the church, I am at the cemetery. They ask me to throw a handful of soil and rose petals on your coffin. The grave is dug deep, and I can see the roots of trees that will sap your essences away. Everything is so unreal, so unbelievable, as if I am in a medieval legend.

I still believe that it was someone else we buried up at Point Claire. That day, the wild nature around us, kookaburras and magpies were flying over the graves. I was looking around, searching for you. "When is Robert coming?" I ask. Friends pat me on the back and hug me. "Where is Robert?" I ask again. I see strange creatures around me. Gorgons, dragons, goblins, griffins, ogres, chimeras. It's like being in a Gustav Mahler song cycle, yes, the *Songs of the Earth*. *Dunkel ist das Leben, ist der Tod*. Dark is life, dark is death. Now our love becomes a hearsay, a ghost, a farewell. And the voice still sings: *Dunkel ist das Leben, ist der Tod*. And I am still surrounded by sinister abysmal creatures, metallic, hungry, menacing. I fainted on your grave. I lost all sense of time. Past, present, future all collapsed. *Ewig... ewig...*

How can I talk about your absence without falling into vapid sentimentalism, without distorting the colors and the music of your existence? You, my high tower, you, my painful lyricism, Achilles and Hamlet together, my companion in the tribulations of being. After thirty years with you, how can I be myself? You gave me my symbols and my mythology. Is there any self to imagine without you? Can I become who I was before you appeared in my life?

I don't go out anymore. I don't want to open the door of our home, fearing that your lingering essence will be swept away by winds and airs. I smell you everywhere. From sunrise to sunset, you are here, and I whisper your matins and vespers. By you, with you and in you, I received my instruction and my creed. I will never be given rest now, my unconscious will take over my being, my iniquities will devour my face. I became so ugly after you left. I started eating and eating like a pig. My body was deformed. My soul regained its fallen nature.

I want to relive your voice, the way you pronounced words, the manner of your body when you uttered them, the gestures of your hands, the specific space you embodied. I try to relive the way you said Sydney, ocean, train, egg, or Britten, song, street, Gubaidulina, Athena, or your own name. Some poets say that we are here to utter words. No, no, no, that's untrue: we are here to listen to words spoken by the lips of those we love. We listen, and all becomes a melody that sings out the real and which we want to recreate in times of distress, when we meet death in the midst of life.

I descended into the darkness of your absence and now I am lost, have no language, cannot announce things, and call them to existence. I can still hear: Sydney, music, Chatswood, gardenia, waratah, Anastasia. It's your voice again. I feel the rain and touch the sun. What you left for me becomes a key and doorway to the Moscows, the Madrids, the New Yorks and the Tokyos we never visited. But that day in Melbourne we looked at each other and said: what will happen if one of us dies first? And the city replied for us with sound and fury. I am in Melbourne now and your face is everywhere, so much so that I am not in Melbourne anymore.

Once upon a time, we were at King's College in Cambridge when the children's choir sang Gabriel Faure's *In Paradisum*; it was in the cold, rainy and misty winter of England, where the contemplation of pure beauty was made possible for us. "That is me," you said, "my true voice," and looked elsewhere. I didn't know what you meant then. Having lost all sense for beauty now, I must live with such glimpses of its presence through my recollections of you. I don't know where we are coming from; I don't know where we are going to. I don't care where birth brought us from; I don't care where death will take us. Life itself is the enemy now. Our friends go on holidays and send photos of lavish dinners and happy dances. Their happy moments bring me to the gates of perdition. It is not envy or resentment, simply a lover's complaint for the lost spring of his soul.

Now that you are gone, I am trying to under-stand what happened during the last thirty years: we met young and beautiful and were cut apart old and infirm. I hear bells tolling at night when our lively suburb goes to bed. One night, I went out following the sound. It was cold, seven degrees, and around midnight. I passed by many churches, but a friend told me that they must have been in my imagination. "Maybe you started having auditory hallucinations," he added. The superstitious child from a small village growing up with the fairy tales and the witch stories of his grandmother had awoken in me again. "I have emigrated to the world of Edgar Allan Poe," I say to myself. We all nurture a sentimental tale reminding us of what is not with us anymore, the poems we first memorized, the faces that illumined our confused youth, the tunes we whistled when we were first left alone in the dark amongst strangers.

You showed me your story. It was written on your body: a deep wound through your chest after an operation in your diaphragm. You were thrown in the same lethal hospital that was to take you away decades later, a nine-year-old boy, alone with older strangers sighing and moaning around you. Visitors were allowed only in the afternoon, so you spent the days and the nights in fear and trembling. You kept mentioning it as the primal dread of your existence. You didn't want anyone to see your scarred chest.

When we met you were afraid to be naked. "My body is horrible," you said. "You will be disgusted by me. I don't understand why you don't leave. I am used to being left alone, to be looked upon with repugnance." That was the great sign of innocence in you. "Don't touch on my chest," you said. "Please don't." And I didn't. Then I said: "I am putting on weight easily. Who wants to be with a chubby Mediterranean?" You laughed. "I will turn fat and burly in my fifties," I said. "It's my ethnic genetics." "Are we going to be together because of our faulty genes?" you wondered. "It seems so," I replied. "Fair enough" you said, and our deep time began at that moment.

"Your eyes," you said, "your eyes, see through me like x-rays. I am dirty, I have done bad things. I wanted to be desired and accepted. Nobody liked me except in the protection of the dark. Hidden areas, dark rooms, and foggy saunas. Every time they looked at my body, they left. Scars everywhere, on my face, my abdomen, my skin. When I turned twenty-five, I tried to commit suicide. I couldn't cope anymore with the cruel lovelessness of my existence. "I have had enough of this horrible lie," I said to myself. But you can see through me, I feel it. From the first time we met, you smiled, and I felt human. Your brought back my childhood, the shadows and joys of those unsuspicious years we all deserve. The lost child of my early life was born in me again. Do you remember what I told you: "You won't leave me? We must make this work!" Then full of doubts: "Why do you want to stay with me? I am not the man for you." This was the second sign of your innocence.

It was naïve to think that only you committed all the meaningless acts that our frustrated generation took on as political duties and social obligations. Growing up in the eighties meant complete disorientation and confusion. We spent the best years of our youth terrified by lethal diseases, name-calling, and the death of our best friends. Clandestine sexual athletics were our escape to the utopian land of freedom. Yet by the time we met, we had had enough sex to know what sex is about. We were frustrated with the humbug and hallucinogenics of orgasmic physicality and the hegemony of hormones. Between sensualism and asceticism we knew how to navigate prudently: we would have enough of both across the different stages of our relationship.

But we could see beyond our instincts and our sublimations. Imperceptibly and rather early, our relationship underwent an ethical transforma-tion: we felt more and more responsible for each other. The passionate cry: "I want you," was transformed into a gentle whisper asking: "Do you want something?" This happened around '96 and grew in depth and scope over the rest of our years. Without realizing it, we had discovered what Albert Camus had called, "the private, fully human world", which constitutes the universal condition as a mixture of affection and routine. And although we were tested by temptation, we subdued it and searched for the mutuality of meaning where grace and empathy blossomed.

Our generation misread Freud, was misled by Marx, was fooled by Sartre, hoodwinked by Marcuse and totally duped by Foucault. So many charlatans promised us liberation and instead we found ourselves mourning our lost friends or being afraid of our own mind, falling prey to depression or narcissism. Some of us opted for drugs, nihilism, suicide. Through the notorious liminal experience, many never found their center. Some realized the delusion, the madness, the big deception. In different parts of the world, you and I, we intuited that we couldn't stop time in flashes of ejaculatory transcendence, and we had to accept the foundation of all foundations, the thoughtful surrender to vulnerability and sorrow.

"I won't complain if you go," you said, "and we do not see each other again." Tears in your eyes, hands shaking. Then, you turned your face away and whispered: "Do not judge me, please." That day I gave you the keys to my apartment. "Why?" you said surprised, "how come? Do you trust me?" "Yes, I do." Then silence. And then you smiled. And I gave you my hand, ritualistically, as befits my dramatic personality. We gave a tacit promise, that's all; the tender touch of our youthful skins struggled to make sense of the challenge: "How are we going to grow old together?" For some moments, for some hours, for some years, it seemed that fear disappeared, dread evaporated, suspicion vanished, and "permanence was possible," as our beloved writer said. "You won't leave me," you whispered. "I cannot leave you," I replied. "You are my home."

The intimacy of small moments, of moments within moments, transformed everything into graceful gestures, guiding us through years and places. The initial passion and fury were slowly transformed into serene moods of mutual absorption. Desire lost its sting, while sexual fantasies, mental role playing, and hyperventilation were quickly and permanently (how should I say this?) stripped naked and simplified. Magically, we ceased being the confused adolescents who didn't know what to do with their bodies. The more we got to know each other, the more our gaze focused on who we were: we never closed our eyes during love. We were looking at each other with desire, piety, and wonder. "You are mine and I am yours," we said. An extension of me, a new me, another being in me.

We helped each other concretize our desires by casting away illusions and adolescent fantasizing. It was yours and no one else's, the body I touched. Everything else, and everyone else, was eclipsed by the fullness of your presence.

Problems emerged, friction and the occasional long silences. Still, we never quarreled, never said bad words, never got angry. We smiled and everything was dispelled in thin air. And yes, I must tell you now, I have forgotten how to make love with anyone other than you. For me, sensuality was a total immersion into the mysteries and the beauty of your existence. We don't live with ghosts, no, but we don't live with substitutes either. Only you and I, my prince, only you and I. You found me. The quest ended then. We were only thirty and the journey ended then. This city brought us together. This city held us together. We breathed each other through our nostrils, like natural elements, like the smell of your flowers, like the fragrances of the urban chaos. This city tore us apart with cruelty and insidiousness, but we loved her because she brought us together, thirty years ago, for a journey that created our life, the only life we could both endure.

One day you said: "I know when you are home from work because I can smell gardenias." I, on the other hand, could feel you coming home because of your rhythmic walking, as if you were reliving the melodies and tunes of your beloved music. "Did you play Puccini's *Crisantemi* today?" I asked once. "How did you know?" you said in surprise. "You were walking with it," I replied. "That's super romantic," you said. "Fully sick." Everyday life was full of such small epiphanies, revealing aspects of our mind we didn't know that existed. To thine own self be true, said the poet. You can be true to yourself only if you attune it to somebody else's being. Your world is doubled, it's a renewed and transfigured world: ultimately, you are more than what you ever imagined or experienced. You enter the stage where the self unfolds its own being consciously, through a surprising and unknown territory, creating the magic mirror that helps us cross onto the other side of reality.

Discovering the other in yourself is painful. Understanding how crucial the other is for your everyday life is also upsetting. You surrender part of your independence and autonomy. In our world, independence might also mean isolation and self-abandonment. You and I knew so many men who were afraid to surrender themselves to each other out of the fear of being betrayed. Most had been ridiculed, profaned, and rejected in their life. In defending their existence, they became individualistic, greedy and fanatical. Their life-styles became defense mechanisms, to satisfy the rule of conformity. They substituted human affection and intimacy with violent outbursts of dark self-oblivion and self-annihilation.

In the beginning, we used to go to bars and pubs along Oxford Street, playing the flirting and seduction games, showing off and testing our success. One night, less than a year after we met, you whispered in my ear while at the Oxford Hotel: "It's time to go home and stay there, don't you think?" The way you pronounced each word was like a religious vow, confirming the bond that would keep us together. It was the simplicity of your sentence that woke in me the primal yearning to belong. I must choose, I thought. This moment for all moments, this man for all men. I looked around and said good-bye to all that – and that was it. I followed you out and we never went back. With your words you created a hearth, around which we could experience each other's history and listen to each other's stories.

From then on, for twenty-nine years, we would remain reconciled with the bewildering world against which we had fought all our youth. "Do you think that we will be accepted?" you asked. "Why would we want to be accepted by those we don't accept?" I replied. "Because they have power," you said. I put my hand on your heart: "This is power, Rob. The rest is nothingness." You gracefully smiled: "Let us be who we are. Let us become who we can be. We cannot live with lies or through illusions, searching for the unobtainable and being content with the fake." The fear of not being accepted vanished. We accepted each other and that was the full story.

We became the complete worlds we were meant to be.

We didn't have to "come out" or release manifestos about our sexuality. We didn't transform ourselves into sociological categories. We didn't minoritize our existence. We never infantilized ourselves with spectral identifications. Life knows no limits, yes, we knew that. But in order to be who we are, we had to come up with our own limits, to impose them on us and consolidate our center. All knew who we were and there was no doubt about the nature of our common life. These things, however, our "erotics," as Mr. Manoly Lascaris would have called them, belonged to us and to nobody else. We didn't want to discuss them publicly, in the same way that our parents never discussed their erotics with others. No pretense, no Peter Pan syndrome, no fear of persecution.

When we went to Athens, they all loved you: my mother, father, siblings and friends. "You are matching each other so nicely," my mother told me. "I will make the bed with my best linen," my auntie said in the humble village where I was born. "They are the silk sheets of my wedding night." For all of them, our relationship was a natural occurrence, an undisputable and inevitable and unbreakable event. Once, I took you to a rough, proletarian tavern outside Athens, to show you the archaic savage Greece, away from the romanticized photographs of classical beauty taken in museums. One of the local villagers, the most macho of all, in his fifties, mustache, white hat, thirties suit and pointed shoes, suspicious of all outsiders, asked me about us. "What is the story between you two?" he said smirking. "We are a couple," I responded, "like you and your wife." "I don't believe you," he said. "You don't look girly." "It depends on the day of the week," I answered. "You try to be smart," he said. "How can I prove it?" I asked. "Kiss him on his lips now in front of us," he shouted for all to hear. Without hesitation, I passionately kissed your elegant lips in front of all those, unknown, wild, uncouth villagers. I thought that they would take their knives out and kill us on the spot. Their reaction, which puzzled and surprised you as much as me, was, after some minutes of dead silence, a prolonged and loud bravo, hands clapping in joy. "You are *dobros*," the macho man said, patting me on the back, using a Slavic word with a long history in Greek. "Really brave lads, palikaria. You look good together." "Yes, we do," I replied. "I like you," he said. "You won't backstab anyone. Only loyalty matters."

That night, we were his guests, and he paid for everything. I didn't translate the verbal exchange to you. "What was all about?" you asked later. "Well, in the beginning, he thought that we were poofters," I explained, "but after I kissed you, he said that we are brave, tough, that we take no bullshit." "What a strange country," you said pensively.

In Hydra, when we visited the Australian house of the Johnstons, the old lady at the hotel reception was equally flattering. "Are you special friends? I don't have a room with a double bed. But I will give you one with two beds and you can push them together to be close to each other. I don't have the heart to separate you, even for a single night." When we left, she gave us the paper icon of the apostles Peter and Paul kissing cheek to cheek to have "their blessings".

Only in your beloved England we faced problems. One time, (do you remember?) it happened at The Wellington pub, when some goons started yelling insults against a foreign male couple and we tried to intervene. They screamed at us. "I will kill you, fucking fag," said one of them. "I'll smash your head and you'll be begging for mercy. I will wait outside and kill you." "Let's go out now, moron," I yelled with all my vocal force. He murmured something and left the pub. He was probably terrified more by my Greek accent than by my physique. I followed him out, ready for anything, but he was nowhere to be seen. "I didn't know that you were so determined," you said. "You make me strong," I replied. "I was defending our Troy."

In a similar vein of bigotry, a nasty priest with whom I discussed our love told me in his sneaky way: "Love is good but don't forget the sins you are committing with him." "Priest," I said with my theological energy in full force, "I know all too well what sin is about: I am baptized, and I am accountable to the one who sent the Holy Spirit when I became a member of His community." He grumbled a bit and said: "May God forgive you." "May God forgive us all according to the sincerity and purity of our heart," I replied. "You are here to console and comfort not to condemn and castigate." He couldn't understand that you were my passage to the abyss of nothingness or to the absolution of universal bliss. Reality works in mysterious ways, sometimes indirectly, other times imperceptibly, and against all expectations. Usually, sin is disguised as redemption; occasionally however redemption is disguised as sin. And who can safely distinguish evil from beauty or goodness from hubris?

Despite such perplexities, we never felt rage or resentment. Strong in our commitment, we faced every challenge from our determination to be who we were, without fear or guilt, persecution mania or social panic. Such incidents paled to insignificance in front of the peak moments of our life together. Our childhood was a struggle with our class and not with our sexuality – that was a common bond between us, above culture, mentality, or language. Yet we remained within the quotidian world of negativity and violence, not hiding behind fake life-styles and ivory towers. We could have done both – but we chose not to. Some are mesmerized by the brokenness of people because they don't want them to be complete. The world of grace however is much morc intriguing than the margins of the terrified or the abyss of the damned.

Our generation produced some many kidults, men and women determined not to grow up but rather live in the constant stimulation of each moment, who, as they grew older, sacrificed their talents to the seductions of self-oblivion. Through the demonic nostalgia for adolescence, depression kicked in, along with self-loathing and rejection. The pathological idea of a puer eternus destroyed their ability to be in the moment and encounter the miraculous unpredictabilities of life. Fantasies, illusions, ghosts displaced the worship of the real and replaced it with evanescent head-trips, phantasms, and delusions. Sadly, we saw the end of many, we witnessed their demise, some were very close friends, the people we grew up with.

"You are so lucky that you found each other," one such friend told us in London. It was 2015. She was a musical celebrity, with spectacular professional success and international fame. Several weeks after our meeting, she hanged herself. "Loneliness is such a swampy lake," she told us when we met at the National Gallery. "I don't want to live in there anymore. I have become successful, have had heaps of men, made money, enjoyed influence, but all this makes me depressed." There was something final and ominous in her voice, but we thought it was because of her nostalgia for Australia. When her death was made known, you were devastated. "I could have saved her," you repeated in distress. But you couldn't. She had planned her destiny. She was of the same age as you. "My generation," you said, "confronts its demons as we approach sixty. And we can find no angels to help us." You never forgot her, the sweet memory of your student years. Till the end you looked after the little plant she gave you back in '97 before leaving Australia. "It's a symbol," you said, "of our years at the Con, the careless days of our youth." And just a few months before you departed you went up to the garden, after dark, looking at the skyline, and said something I didn't understand then. "Goodbye, Debby, we will meet soon." "Are you talking to yourself?" I asked in my utter silliness. "No," you replied, "Only to Debby. To my youth." Your friends, your friends meant so much to you. Every Christmas, you would decorate our home with flickering lights, a small tree with a star, and place presents around it on the floor for your friends. You bought inconspicuous, elegant gifts, small and beautiful objects. I still have some of them. Recently, I found four small gifts you had for Debby. You never had the chance to give them to her, to your youth.

⌒

I was happy, very happy indeed, before meeting you. I was delighted when I travelled, when I read good books, being an irresponsible and untroubled vagabond. I never felt abandoned or excluded. I still remember the feeling of being alone and self-sufficient with the Inuit in Canada or with the Samis and their aurora borealis up in Finland.

Only after me met, aloneness was disconnected from self-sufficiency. Only through you, I became identical with my unfolding self and the union of opposites was realized in me. Such gluing can be done by another person. A relationship does not always aspire to happiness, but rather to enduring time together. We never become who we are by ourselves; our beliefs betray our need for communion; our politics misrepresent our existence; our actions falsify our mind. Only through the grace of another's gaze, in some privileged moments, the image of our completed existence emerges, our character is molded, masks melt away and we see our face. We look at it, we recognize it, we are awed and distressed, we try to capture it, we fail, and then, time goes and it is no more. I was faceless before we met: you gave me my face by looking at me. Your departure left me without a distinct reality, my own mode of seeing. The cruel way you escaped into nothingness hollowed out everything. Empty shells everywhere. Only silence now, and silence is all. Now you belong to someone else. And I belong to something else, beyond me, beyond me.

I look around and all your beloved objects stand still while dancing in a frenzy of memories. I remember when you bought that painting, where we found that scarf, the places you bought your shoes, vests, gloves, watches, shirts, cufflinks, toys, red London busses. Each one brings back the streets, the people we met, the discussions we had: these trivial moments flashed in your eyes when you were unable to see and yet are what really remains in us till the last moment of our conscious existence. Rome, London, Edinburgh, Venice, Paris, Athens, Melbourne, Adelaide. "Do you remember the unreality of St Peter's in Rome?" you once asked. "We felt so lost in there. Until we saw Michelangelo's *Pietà*, and the whole universe became palpable and concrete." "Yes," I replied, "the most important sculpture of faith, in a dark corner, pushed aside." We stood in front of it for hours: would it be strange to say that at that moment I was both the mother who cried and the son who suffered? And that in a strange way, your body has been connected to that statue? And that when you were lying in the hospital, I thought that you were like that son who died in pain, and I was your mother trying to protect you from death? O, the mind, the mind has depths, that imagine to be mountains.

During your final days, I was sleeping next to you in the hospital room, and in the dark of the night you were talking about all such scattered and inexplicable encounters: that strange seller of green leather gloves in Venice, who looked like an alchemist; the peculiar woman in Edinburgh castle and her scarves, who looked at the lines of your palm in horror and said: "You don't have long to live"; the strange Englishman in Athens who came on to you and asked "Are you up for some fun tonight?" "Do you remember?" you said, from your hospital bed, "You were so jealous." Yes, I was. "Do you remember the Clinton visit to Athens and the demonstrations?" We went out after hearing the police sirens and saw the Molotovs hurled from all over the place, burning cars, garbage bins and shops. "A fiery apocalypse," you said. "What a mess." The whole city in a state of war. But you were more impressed by something else: "Did you hear how the Greek presidential orchestra played the national anthem of the United States? It was as if they didn't know how to play music. It sounded like Kylie Minogue!" "Welcome to the land of almost-there and so what," I responded. "You must get used to it." But you didn't, always exploring it in bafflement and wonder.

We talked about some of these little incidents in our last week together. We were not laughing then, but that last night they were moments of pure transparency when life was spreading its bewildering and seductive web on our mind in the midst of pain and anguish. It was upsetting and disturbing and transformative. "I've had enough," you said, at the moment when the horrible nurses were injecting you with more and more morphine. "I am a goner," you added with your usual Australian melancholy. "Why are you giving him so much morphine?" I asked. Only then, I realized that something was seriously wrong. We were holding hands and leaning our heads gently against each other. That Saturday night we talked about everything: our fears, desires, indiscretions. You even told me in the dark the word we had avoided using between us. "Vras," you whispered, "I never told you how much I love you… It's love," you said, "I have felt it since the day we met. Love, oh yes, love, is the simple word I was looking for these last thirty years, but I couldn't find it. Or maybe it was always on my tongue but didn't want to misuse it." You never did, my prince. Love is the word that hides many sins, much malice and horrible self-deception. You loved in deed and in truth through your whole existence. You gave yourself unconditionally to me, the fallible, the faithless and the fool; only your trust was enough to transform our bond into a fellowship of innocence and redeem the purity of us, the misguided children of this century.

We always avoided the sentimentalism of grand statements, so common and so hackneyed in these days of emotional prolixity. A touch, a glance, a gesture was enough to reaffirm the bond: we would grow old together. Irrespective of any prejudice or acceptance. Irrespective of any difference or ambition. Despite all temptations or obstacles. "You never tried to change me. I was really grateful for your respect," you whispered. No, I didn't want replicas of myself or projections of my ideal ego. When we disagreed, we usually kicked each other on the foot, or simply said, "Stop being silly now". It was so inspiring to avoid defining what we were actually doing.

In the nights before your departure, you kept talking about music. "It's a pity I won't play Brahms' *A German Requiem*, again," you said. I remembered the day you played it at the Opera

House, back in 2002; your excitement, your near-religious transfiguration. When the sublime and tragic lamentation was heard in the second movement, *Denn alles Fleisch, es ist wie Gras, / So seid nun geduldig / Denn alles Fleisch, es ist wie Gras…* I saw tears in your eyes, your hands shaking on the viola, looking desperately around for a friendly face to hold you back in this world of infinite imperfections. And you looked at me. I was far back at the concert hall but nodded with reverence and assent. There was no distance between us. You were far away but I could feel your heartbeat and absorb your body warmth. Yes, all flesh is like grass, we knew it, after my brother Nicholas died, your father Alex died, your mother Marie died, and my mother Anastasia departed. We didn't have enough time to mourn each one of them. They disappeared from our life like the green grass of the *Requiem* and we didn't even have the opportunity to revisit their graves, recollect their existence or ask for their forgiveness.

Once, I went by myself to the Orthodox Church in Newtown and asked the priest if he could say a prayer for their souls. "You can do it yourself," the good priest said. "Read whatever you want. You have my blessing." I read Psalm 88, the relevant chapter from Paul's *Thessalonians*, and Rilke's *Ninth Duino Elegy*. I felt complete, more human, more myself, more, us. You were in hospital then. "You should have invited me too," you said, "so we could call them back to life together." Then the pernicious lockdowns came, the panic and the confusion. The strange reality of isolation and the collapse of all rational order in the hospital system. I couldn't even bring you food, your toothbrush, fresh clothes. You were calling me from your mobile: "They will undo me," you said. "They treat me like a leper in complete isolation." I tried to intervene and then I witnessed the cruel impenetrability of the system. When you came out, around the end of August 2021, you had lost twenty kilos, and you would not recover. You had nine months to live.

In the dark of the last nights the feeling of finality was all around us; palpable, overpowering, unrelenting. Soft light from the window transformed the beloved features of your face into strongholds against the shadows of the underworld. We tried not to cry. "This moment feels like a consummation to me," you said. "Keep me in your mind if you can." As everything was slipping away, we realised how fertile and deep our years together had been. We were euphoric to be together at the crossroads of cultures and societies: you saved me from the sterile deserts of academia, and I offered you the open horizons of an outsider. Home, that's home, when time slows down and space is elongated, when the presence of deep emotion disrupts the continuum of everydayness and destabilises the habits that make life opaque and meaningless. "You brought me so much light," you said. "You gave me so much clarity," I responded. Then silence. The moment was ripe, and time stood still. Suddenly, an unknown voice called us back to reality, a nurse, perhaps, an angel maybe, and love shook our heart like an ancient Greek poem with its simplicity and truth.

Life is a constant loss of innocence. The enemy is not death; it's untimely death. The feeling that we have not completed what we could have completed. We are afraid of dying because we may not have even begun the most important things we wanted to achieve. Many live their lives as in perpetual parentheses. Waiting for the real things to happen while being consumed by the distractions of everyday existence. Untimely death, the lost horizon of transfiguration, that's what my mourning and my grief are about. The sadness and the sorrow of early departure mean nothing when you have completed your cycle and have realised your transformation, when you could have pronounced your own triumphant, "It is accomplished." What can we accomplish in our today toing-and-froing of specular un-realities and frustrating illusions?

The unintended consequence of love is the concretisation of our being. You helped me crystalise who I am. I probably did the same for you. From the immense bundle of desires, whims, and impossibilities I was made of before we met, you gave me a point of convergence, the moment of self-recognition, the centre. It was so natural and seamless; beyond all description. The birds know nothing about the air they fly through. Neither the fish about water. Nor humans about their soul. They escape into its luminous night in moments of existential peril and come out in instants of emotional surrender.

⁓

Half of our lives were spent next to each other, with the ups and downs of a shared existence and the problems of everyday banality. But your kindness, the generosity, and gentleness of your presence transformed everything. No ambiguities, no ambivalence, no "I love you and I hate you." We travelled together around the world, we watched the same movies, read the same books. The old idea that friendship is one soul in two bodies was achieved. Serenity is the word. This was what we offered each other. The feeling of collectedness, and presence of mind; no dichotomies, divisions, split selves, or disjunctions. We were at the place we wanted to be, with the person we wanted, and all was well. Do I idealize you? Maybe. I really cannot discern the line between what happened and how it happened. In an era of escapist fantasies, I need to think mythically about you, against the languages of death that prevail, and darken the mind, ruling our everyday world.

I met you as a freelance musician struggling to book new gigs. Your life was full of music. Elgar, Britten, Delius, Barber, Walton, all the British tradition, which you adored and rehearsed constantly. I remember your quartet, Crisantemi, with Petra, Debby and Dominique. You were meeting every day at our flat in Glebe, rehearsing, perfecting and fine-tuning your music.

For almost five years you worked hard and constantly. "I don't know how good I am," you said, "but I want to become better."

When in 2004 you decided to become a teacher, your new self emerged: motivated, creative, constructive, and positive. Your studies were both exciting and exhausting. Your anxiety to learn how to make PowerPoint presentations was matched by your need for self-reflection. I bought two bottles of Veuve Clicquot to celebrate your new beginning. "We will drink it," you said, "when I graduate." You immersed yourself in study with genuine dedication and confusion. Four years later, we cracked open the champagne. We went to Bondi and in front of the wine-dark sea, we had it lavishly with fish and chips. It was a beautiful December after-noon, and for some reason, inexplicable to this day, we remained silent. I still remember the humming of the bubbles in the plastic cups, the seagulls trying to steal our chips, the gentle breeze from the sea as the sun was going away.

We stayed till very late on the beach. We didn't say a word. It was a farewell and a welcome. When we returned home to Glebe, the small balcony of our apartment was full of lorikeets and parrots. "What is the meaning of all these?" you wondered out loud. "It is like being in a painting by De Chirico." And his is how your new life began and its final chapter was inaugurated.

For over ten years, you woke up at six in the morning to be at school by seven in order to prepare the music stands for the kids. At Chatswood Public School you established one of the largest music programs in the state, receiving awards and accolades. Yet you were always modest and reserved; you disliked taking credit for what was a collective effort. Those of us who heard the music performed by 100 and more students under your baton caught the wave of your generosity and sharing. Your students were visibly inspired by your enthusiasm and the performances were of the highest quality even by the standards of adult musicians.

It was at that moment, when your full creative potential was blossoming, that the first tragedy struck. One night you came back home with your left eye red and teary. We immediately rushed to the Eye Hospital at the center of our city. We waited at the emergency ward for two, four, six hours. We were sent back home, with some eyedrops, and asked to come back the next day. By then, the infection had progressed beyond any possible cure. "We cannot identify the virus," doctors said. And they sent you to the Prince of Wales Hospital where you had one of the most horrible experiences of your life. Manic nurses who refused to give you Panadol, psychopathic doctors who claimed an inability to do anything, elderly patients screaming for their dead mother in Croatia all night. Physical pain became mental anguish.

Over the course of two weeks, the infection destroyed your eye, which would have to be removed. "It is a few inches from the brain," they said. "If it goes deeper, that will be the end." Three months in hospital, suffering in agony. You came out mutilated but didn't give up. You took on the hospital and successfully argued your case of criminal negligence. You were so happy when you won the case. We celebrated at a Thai restaurant in Newtown. Last time we went out together. We walked slowly back home. You were happy. Now I see again everything that happened when we were going back home. Your smile, your face, your sense of satisfaction. We stopped at a Buddhist center, a vegan restaurant, a secondhand bookshop, a nursery, a supermarket. We bought bread, vegemite, milk, butter and ice-cream. Slowly, slowly, we walked back home. You had forgotten your keys and we had to use mine to open the security door. When we entered our apartment, you took out your viola and frantically played your favorite sonata by Benjamin Britten. I was entranced and spellbound. "This can't be real," I said to myself. "We will be punished for this."

I remember the first time we walked together after you were discharged. In a moment of panic, you whispered in absolute horror: "I cannot see anything, everything is blurred and foggy." You clung on to me with despair and dread. "Take me back home, Vras, take me back home. I see nothing, I am blind." I put my arm around your waist to guide you gently back home where you crashed on the sofa speechless and horrified. You spent almost two months isolated at home until one morning you said, "Vras, you need a haircut," and smiled in happiness. December 2017: "Your Bolognese is disgusting." "I made it especially for you with expensive French red wine," I protested. "Yet it is still disgusting," you insisted smirking with happiness. "We are here," you added. "It is enough. I will survive your disgusting cooking." I wish I could live those moments again.

You went back to school and with your diminished eyesight you struggled to teach music for another two years. I read so many testimonials about you over that time, end-of-year letters that held deep expressions of gratitude. Then, in 2018, the leukemia suddenly surfaced. With broken heart you had to stop teaching and gradually leave school altogether.

For the last three years of your life, time was divided between home and hospital, as you were getting increasingly weaker. The disease advanced and no treatment could stop it. In 2021, the chronic lymphocytic leukemia mutated to aggressive Hodgkin's lymphoma. "Only the five per cent of patients suffer this," said the doctor. Then new Covid restrictions were imposed, turning the already grim situation into a farce with tragic consequences. You were the collateral casualty of a collective panic and a mass hysteria.

Everyday life for you became agonizing, full of medications with horrible side effects. The decline started then, although some moments of immense clarity, beauty and grace were given to both of us. A magnificent full moon in January over Sydney, the blossoming waratah in our garden, your meetings with old friends from the school days in the 70s, especially Paula, who infused you with the incurable optimism of your adolescence. I feel so grateful for these simple moments of transparency and beauty that emerged from under the fear of death. Then, hospital again, where your beautiful mind started becoming agitated, unsettled and confused. "We have something beautiful together," you told me in a moment of clarity. "Remember me, I have suffered so much but I love our garden, I love music and teaching." Musician, teacher, friend: that what I inscribed on your tombstone.

Two weeks before you left, we were planning how to vote in the elections. You were alert and active. Things declined fast, and on the last night of your life you were hallucinating, you were restless, you were mumbling broken words. "I need an explanation," you were saying, looking at me in the dark. "What happened? Why? I deserve an explanation. We must buy that small house on the Greek island. I want to see Crete and go to Scotland." Then silence. You started breathing heavily. I was holding your hand. I could feel the anger and frustration. I could sense the rage at being dependent on somebody. In the morning, your beloved cousins Deborah and Suzan arrived. I left for an hour, and you breathed your last breath. You didn't die alone as you were afraid. Sue and Deb formed around you the sacred chorus of psychopomps.

At night, dreams chase me relentlessly. There is a recurring one, which upsets me the most. I am looking for you around Sydney, which is covered in dark clouds. As I turn at the corner of George and Paramatta roads, I find myself in Chile. I am in Santiago Central Station waiting for the train to Patagonia. It is 1988. Early July. I have made this trip because I want to stay permanently in the land of Pablo Neruda. I was offered a position at the university. "I will stay here forever," I reassure myself. A raven flies over me, the train stops, I am in a state of panic, lost somewhere in the endlessness of time and materiality, and suddenly I confront the events of my unlived future. I never went to Australia. I never met Robert Meader. Never worked at Sydney University. I stayed in Chile. I spoke Spanish and not English. I repeated hundreds of times the immortal words: *Dos amantes dichosos hacen un solo pan*... Then the train comes, I hop in and find myself in Woy Woy, the very first day you took me there to meet your mother. As we talk, we hear Jessie Norman singing 'Frühling' from Richard Strauss' *Four Last Songs*, over the Brisbane Water, the same song we heard before your last admission to hospital.

I wake up and there is a storm over Sydney. In our bedroom, your clothes are everywhere. The rain falls endlessly. On the ceiling, shadowy reflections from the outside world stare at me.

Thunder and lightning interrupt the tense silence. It rains for days and nights, I am alone in bed, I wish we could see all tempests together, in silence and awe. After you left, I lost my ability to admire and feel wonder. Now I live with shadows and noises, no bodies, no material bliss, no earthly delights.

I plundered your garden and now I must live through an immense desert, in the middle of the city, a desert of sorrow, in a constant rebellion against myself, listening to the groaning within me, lost and sinful and without horizon. Sometimes, fantasies jump out of my brain and look like truth: we have just had sex, a one-night stand, and then forgotten each other. We have returned to the mad life of promiscuity and self-forgetting. But the airy nothingness of illusions evaporates, and I am next to our beloved things, a crying self, laughing at my own face, scolding my own stupidity and submission to the idols of today. All was good, everything that happened was providential: we were two little worlds who achieved their existence by living the soundless and uneventful life of two ordinary men in love.

Self-pity? Joan Didion talks a lot about this. I have never felt self-pity; it has nothing to do with you. You stood dignified and smiling till the end, the true Stoic that you never wanted to be. Self-pity doesn't appear in the equation of your departure. Your memory transcends my petty ego, even my melancholia, my dark visions of rage and destruction. I didn't do enough to save you: that's what I feel. I should have been more active, more inquisitive and aggressive. I should have asked my friend at Oxford to invite you for their experimental treatment for Hodgkin's lymphoma. Or asked for help from my cousin in Greece, who is researching a possible cure.

Your doctors were so indifferent and inhuman and evasive. "Oh, you are so much part of our family," one of them said at some point, then didn't even call to express condolences. The system and its protocols seemed more important than the humans it was supposed to help. "There are many lines of defence against this," they told us at the start. Then, in less than a year, they exhausted them all. I thought that they knew what they were doing, and I showed too much complacency. I was so wrong. I should have been more demanding. The nurses' story always ended with the same terrible statement: "We work under Covid restrictions. We can do no more." They simply followed "rules and regulations," without realising the danger that your body was nurturing. "Why didn't you tell me," I asked afterwards, "that there were no treatments left, that his lungs were hollowed out by pneumonia, that he didn't respond to any treatment, that there was nothing it could be done?" I showed so much trust. I was thinking of you, however. "Don't become loud," you said. "I have always lived noiselessly. I learned to endure and carry on."

I passed through the Royal Prince Alfred Hospital the other day. For the last four years, it had been something of a second home to us. You suffered so much in there. You were greatly humiliated in there. You reached the end of your tether in there. "I will jump off the last floor," you said once. "I've had enough," you said. My sister died in here, from an undiagnosed blood clot, back in 1990. One day, after a minor operation, the doctors announced her death to us and just left. We entered her room where she was lying cold and lonely and didn't know what to say. The night before, she was up and active and, in the morning, gone. The doctors simply said, "We didn't notice the clot, which went straight to her heart." You talked again and again about her. Every time you entered that hospital you felt her presence. "I cannot enter this building without seeing her," you said. "She looks at me with compassion and affection. 'Oh, my little brother' she says. 'We will meet soon, even though we will never meet again.' This is what I hear every time I enter this building."

I was with you for so many nights in that awful and haunted abode. The nurses mistreated you.

They looked at you with fear. They looked at us with disdain, and contempt, a mixture of ageism and homophobia intensified by an inferiority complex. We felt it so many times. "I would rather die," you said once. "I am more fed up with them than the illness. They are the cancer that will take away my life." I slept next to you for weeks just to take you to the bathroom, clean your body sometimes, change your clothes time and again, ask for extra medication. "I am so ashamed. I am imposing so much on you," you said. Yet I was falling in love with your vulnerability, the fragility of your lean and tall body, with your deep self-respect and dignity in front of the frightening realisation that you couldn't clean yourself. "You must go, Vras", you said. "You must leave me. I will destroy your career, I will be your downfall." Still, I was falling deeper in love with the brittleness of your skin.

One night around eleven you rang the bell for the nurse at least ten times. Thirty minutes passed and no one appeared. "Can you take me to the toilet," you asked. "Please help me. I can't do it myself." I was in a state of trance almost, reverence and piety, as I took your body in my hands and gradually led you into the bathroom. "Thank you," you sighed, and we both were in unseen tears. When a nurse finally came, she made your bed and changed your clothes and left mumbling and complaining. I took your hand and held it in the dark. "It is like the Pieta," I whispered. "This is what it's all about. That's why we are born: to live through such profound moments of helplessness and dependency." "This is what it is all about," you agreed. "Your mother taught me this," I added. Marie Meader, the most gentle and ethereal person I have ever met. It was on the tenth of May, 2019. Exactly three years before you left.

You came out of the trouble then, and we travelled to Melbourne and to Adelaide. We saw movies together and watched German series on television. "I feel an affinity with the German language," you said. "It was my first exit from

Australia back in '86." We were on one such trip, in Melbourne, when my mother Anastasia died in Athens. End of June 2019. I had to rush back and perform the last rites. I buried her, as I had promised, to her native village, next to the house where she spent her childhood. "You must do the same for me," you said. "Take me to Woy Woy and bury me close to my mother and sister and father. The circle will be complete. Back together again." "We are both orphans now," we laughed melancholically. "Our only family is us."

We did not now that we had only two lean years left to experience that terrible and liberating truth. During this time, you had to sell your home in Woy Woy. Alone, you took all the memories of a family out to Vinnies, alone you posted the remaining objects to your brother and alone you farewelled the childhood home of happiness and chaos.

The traumas of the past came through with each object you disposed of. One night you carefully showed me a knife wrapped in a towel. "What is this?" I asked. You were visibly shaken by its presence. You looked around just in case somebody might overhear. "With this knife I threatened my father back in '79," you said, and your face became red. "He was drunk and was about to punch my mother, who was hiding behind a chair crying out for help. I clutched the knife and screamed: 'Get out of here, otherwise I will stub you to death.' I didn't know that I had so much strength in me. He was terrified and left. The police came and issued a restraining order against him. I forced my mother to get a divorce as soon as possible. I have never forgotten the incident. Since that day, I have kept the knife hidden in a safe place. It is a symbol of the day I killed my childhood."

Our parents, the enigmas of our life, we carry them in us. They had children while they were children themselves, unable to grow up. Our parents, the fearsome deserts of our existence. They are lurking in every turn of our life, and they always have new surprises, even though they are dead. We remember them even when we must forget them: we are all born and reside in humble Bethlehems and not all of us are seduced by Jerusalem or Rome.

In your melancholic green eyes, I could detect the most heartbreaking question that all Anglo-Australians, hide, disguise or evade. What are we doing here? This is the burning question that I felt in you and your family. Your great-grandfather and grandmother were transported to these shores in 1834 and '35, for stealing a loaf of bread and a ribbon. They were sentenced to fifteen years hard labour at the penal colony. They were thrown into this unknown land and knew not what to do. "They lost their bearings," you said, "they had to work like slaves, they were mocked and derided by the Protestant overlords, the men became alcoholics and the women were treated like witches. Panic, horror and dismay." In a strange way, I could still detect these emotions in you. "Us Catholics were persecuted for decades," you used to tell me. "We couldn't go to church on Sunday, we couldn't celebrate in public. My grandfather could not do anything with his life because of his faith." You never forgot that. You were always talking about your ancestors. What are we doing here? We belong somewhere else, and we are uprooted by the perfidious hand of power.

In the long run, I understood how painful this truth is, my friend. Every generation thinks that they are something special; that history begins with them, that everything belongs to them, that nothing happened before them. You published the memoirs of your grandfather, *Making Music*, in which he narrated his life in the early twentieth century. It was your great tribute to the ancestors. "Do you know", you asked me, "that until the fifties, Catholics were not allowed to enter pubs and hotels in the countryside?" No, I didn't.

Back in 2004, your mother told me that before dying she wanted to go back "home." I was surprised and asked where her home was. "Up there," she replied, "between Scotland and Ireland." One of your "heart's burning desires" was to visit that place "up there." Many decades later and the certainty that there was a home waiting for you "between Scotland and Ireland" fascinated me. Us latecomers have more or less ignored the Catholic working class convicts whose memory you were so proud of. "If something happens to me, I would like a Catholic burial," you said, "like my mother, my sister and our forefathers." I followed your instructions. The end was given as you asked. At St Joseph's Church, in Newtown. Surrounded by old, musty, and magnificent wooden statues pre-dating the Second Vatican. I even managed to squeeze some Latin into my eulogy: *In articulo mortis caelitus mihi vires.* Latin is the ultimate language of God. After he struggled with Hebrew and Greek, he settled everything in Latin. Only the language of the Romans could bring out my grief, and bring you nearer to him. *Dirige nos domine ad augusta per angusta sic itur ad astra excelsior.* "In my final moments, heavens will give me strength. Guide us, Lord, through trial to triumph which is the path to the stars ever upwards." I thought that your ancestors would have loved this and would have blessed us both.

I remember your anxiety when you took me to the Crypt of St Mary's Cathedral. You wanted me to understand that this was not a work of triumphalism but of extreme dignity, of the reassertion of the right to exist and be visible. As we were walking down the steps to the marble cavern, with its magnificent Celtic Cross and majestic green, yellow, purple and white slabs, you talked about the persecuted Catholics, as if they were your immediate friends and siblings. "People tend to forget this," you said again. "And now there is no home anywhere for us except this place, where we were thrown to die, and we survived by becoming criminals. What redemption can we find and what forgiveness can we be granted?" I was deeply moved by this: you helped me throw away the narcissism of exclusive victimisation, from which so many of us suffer. It is only by being firmly rooted in the faith of your ancestors that you can be unafraid of yourself. All fallen leaves are swept away by the winds of inevitability and each one experiences an identity demolition. We never went through such self-indulgence and self-extinction. Together we were ourselves, separately we were the generation of leaves that Homer talked about; dry, isolated and expelled from the garden of their origin.

In the eve of the new millennium, you performed with the Orchestra of Colors in Athens for the dawn of the new century. You played the melancholic tunes of Manos Hatzidakis on the slopes of the volcano in Santorini. After the recording we walked to the highest promontory of the island and watched the sun descending with all its luminous majesty. "Is it possible?" you asked. "Is it possible for me to be here, now, with you, so far away from my motherland, experiencing the happiness that time can only rarely give us?" Sometimes, I know, the generosity of life overwhelms us. We ask for few good things and are flooded by plenty.

On my death bed, you will hover over me, young and beautiful and radiant, like that afternoon when we watched the sunset over the Aegean, and the sun enormous and vociferous, standing still for hours before vanishing into the horizon, and us looking in amazement and awe. That time, you said, "We are happy now, this is happiness, this is eternity, this is you and I, we will never live this ever again, it has given us a serene feeling of timelessness, a tangible perception of beauty which we have never experienced before in the realms of desolation and noise we inhabited since our birth. All our life was a preparation for this moment. All our future life will be its afterglow." December 29th, 2000, Santorini, at the edge of a ruined medieval castle, with our feet dangling over the abyss. I remained silent and looked at your soft face, your dreamy eyes, your elegant lips, your El Greco fingers, until the sun disappeared, and its light vanished, but you stood there, almost levitating, luminous and transfigured, religious beyond religion, surrounded by the blue sea and the gentle breeze and my childhood memories and the idealisations of my youth, and at that moment all life became suddenly meaningful, transparent, and spiritual.

"Where am I?" I wondered. "Where am I? Time and space have lost their sting, their strength to devour human flesh." Oh, yes, at that inexplicable moment, we had conquered time, we had outgrown our biography, as we looked at the sun diving down the depthless Mediterranean and wished we were diving into the night together. "I am grateful for this moment and for what this land has offered me," you said as we watched the fiery ball dangling over the endless blue. "Maybe we are here, to simply say how grateful we are for everything, without fear or rage, arrogance or malice." I grasped your hand then, and we looked together towards the depths of the Mediterranean horizon; and it was enough to remember that blueness, years later and smile and smile, under the darkest circumstances as chemotherapy was destroying your body.

Years later, we were travelling from England to Scotland and the Isle of Skye, by bus and train. Your dream to find that land "between Scotland and Ireland" was still strong in you. We stopped at a village and as we stepped out, it started snowing heavily. I still remember its name, Callander, almost empty and totally closed although it was just after noon. We were standing one meter apart, but the snow was so heavy that we couldn't see each other. Then surrounded by the thick curtain of ice you leaned gently over me and whispered: "I have never seen snow falling before." I thought I saw tears in your eyes as we stared at the white veils together. "I wish that this would never end," you said. The snow was falling, dense and cryptic, and suddenly, in an eruption of the lurking unfathomable, you started yelling and dancing, you fell on the white ground and mumbled words I couldn't understand. I could simply hear "Yes… yes… yes…" and nothing else. It was a moment of primitive joy, of cosmological exhilaration, the same that the first humans must have felt, after they freed themselves from the shackles of Eden. Sometimes, I know, the generosity of life overwhelms us. We ask for very few things and we drown in plenty.

Several days before your departure we were planning to revisit the village. Now that you are gone, I don't want to do it. I don't want to do it by myself. I will never visit again the places we went together. They belong to you. They will bear forever the traces of your passage, intimations of your existential gleam. Even after we are gone, your presence will be felt as the snow will be falling, and life will go on. Our most beautiful deeds are already forgotten. The best things in us will be forgotten. They existed because we were together. I reclaim silence now, non-existence, my pre-natal life. I contradict myself, I know, Rob, and although I do not contain multitudes, I will contradict myself again and again.

I miss you; everything boils down to this simple sentence.

Some months ago, we were standing together by the mesmerising sea in Sydney, you were made of birds and wind and salt, your face gathering the storm of the coming night, like the souls of people lost in shipwrecks and unforgiving adventures. You were already far away, I could sense it, travelling in the heart of a silver fish and the eyes of an omnipotent bird, looking beyond the horizon, beyond my gaze, far beyond my desire, far beyond the living. In my mind, at that moment, you became the moment, the myriad sounds of a passing aeroplane, of cars driving to nowhere, the sand, the wind, the fallen leaves, the ocean murmur, all elements moving away, whirling around, falling down, going upwards, where the stars absorb our existence and dance our presence and so down here, we remain, empty, oblivious and hungry while in the distant horizons, the angels of our demise chuckle and flap their wings in dismay. It happened just on January 17th, your birthday, on Brighton beach, I have a photograph of us there. As a gift, I gave you the first American edition of Patrick White's *The Vivisector*. You were so happy. You had collected all first American editions of his works and read them for the "sheer pleasure of their paper," despite the pain and restlessness. "I finished reading the novel. It was so cruel and so sublime," you said, only two days before I called the ambulance to take you to hospital.

You never came home again. Hurtle Duffield was your angel for the passage. "Art is the yearning for farewell," you said when they took you to the ambulance. "Bring me some clothes later," you added, "although I don't think I will need them." You looked around, you told me to look after the dogs and to keep the place clean. "Water the plants, but do not overdo it," you said. The door closed behind you and that was the last time I saw you standing up. Because of Covid restrictions, I couldn't come with you. The deafening silence of absolute emptiness, darkness and despair weighed on me. I was crushed, an insect on the floor, a dirty cockroach underfoot. "He is gone," I cried, "he will never be back. He will never see our home again. My home is gone." I passed out and came back to myself hours later. The sun was rising when I rushed to the hospital. "You are not allowed to visit," the security guards told me. I stayed there circling around the building like a shark. I stayed there for hours. I tried your mobile but no answer. Around midday, I walked up to Newtown and silently entered St Joseph's Church. I sat on a pew at the back and, without thinking, whispered a garbled prayer: "My lament is for my love; be near me, eternal void, I call you out of the depths, keep my heart warm, make my soul light, I am engulfed by the waves of the netherworld, I am thrown into the depths of darkness, I want to fly, I want to see your face, my mother abides in it and Robert, the man I love." We all revert to dirges about our powerlessness and misery and weakness when we enter churches. Our despair becomes our prayer.

I was exhausted and fell asleep and had a dream at the church pew, which was real and heavy, and not really a dream. I saw you burying me, preparing my funeral, delivering a heartfelt eulogy. I felt happy: my wish was fulfilled. You know, death causes panic to those who are not ready. I was ready. I have been ready for years. I knew what I wanted to do and did it in the best way possible. What is left incomplete and broken will remain incomplete and broken. My fractured self will never be mended. There were so many gaps in my life, so much dust, good luck and existential clutter. I emptied myself of all my talents and abilities. I became nothing because I did what I could do. You were not ready, I knew it. You started late and needed several years of work and integration to achieve the absolute purity of your existence. The great vivisector didn't give you that gift of time. He separated us at the most beautiful, ripest moment of your being, when you started making tangible the ultimate promise you embodied.

Yet, after your passing, it was I who had to perform the horrible and redeeming funeral rites, search for the grave, give an insipid eulogy, struggle not to cry, force myself to smile, look around with gratitude while I was in utter numbness. I was far away, all voices were coming from a horrible distance, I couldn't hear clearly what they were saying. I couldn't even recognise faces, I couldn't even talk to our friends. We simply hugged each other. I could do nothing except sigh and repeat mechanically, "We must meet soon, we must meet soon." Yet other things were devouring my mind. Ghosts were howling and screaming. "I should be in that coffin", I was thinking. "Why am I out here? Where is Robert? Robert, where are you?"

In death we dissolve like grains of salt; nobody knows that we have been here, nobody remembers our sunny days, a dark tombstone marks the shipwreck of our existence, pure oblivion covers our past. At night, friends mourn our absence, searching for traces of our passing through their world, looking at old photographs, telling stories about us, funny and silly and innocuous, exorcising death and fear, reconciling themselves with the mysterious blackness that follows us like a shadow. Numinous birds in moonless nights and who can see them? Black stars in the formless firmament and who can detect them? And again, who looks at the dark skies when the luminous earth infects us with so many secrets?

In Glebe, ages ago, in a cold winter's night, when the wind was howling wildly, and we were intimate, receiving the ultimate gifts of sensuality, in that sleepy after-moment when the gates between the worlds are slightly lifted, we had our first encounter with the numbness of the beyond. "So that's it," you said, "nothing after this, nothing?" "But isn't this quite a lot?" I said naively, "too much, exhausting and disempowering, beyond endurance sometimes? Nothing, what is this nothing?" I was rationalizing and wanted to keep the fear away. We never talked about this nothing again. We were complete together. We never thought of separating or giving space to each other or looking for some time alone so that the fear of nothing could find place to emerge.

This is how that nothing was suspended, for some time at least. We simply had to be us, neither searching for a self nor fantasizing about an ideal partner. No pretenses, no pretexts, no mirages. We helped each other become who we were. And it was also probably the most that any relationship can do. And yes, we remained faithful to our promise. Sometimes it was hard and in two occasions I was guilty of a serious loss of self-control.

For several weeks, I was infatuated with a Portuguese doctor called Camillo. I had met him before you, but just a few days before you and I met, he had to go back to his country. He came back three years later, and we met unexpectedly in front of the Town Hall. You had sensed it and you said twice, "You are not here with me now. Is everything fine?" I avoided any answer. For two weeks, the silences between us grew. I would not sit next to you on the couch and avoided all physical contact. You understood that something was happening when I ordered food instead of preparing it for us. "You ordered pizza," you said in disbelief. "Something is happening. Pizza means guilt." I told you everything some days later. You held my hand and said, "Do as you please, but don't forget our promise." Ultimately, I didn't forget a thing.

Years later you told me about your own infidelity. "It went on for some months and was abruptly interrupted," you said. "It was purely instinctual," you said, "physical, sexual." I was hurt but I didn't want to know more. In a way, I felt satisfied: my presence didn't isolate you from others. I was not the best lover anyway.

The drama of such minor events brought the catharsis to our grand narrative – it served its purpose, and it was probably necessary to bring us closer, to make us feel what we would be losing if he had gone down that path. More importantly, we never apologized to each other or asked for forgiveness. We didn't resist temptation because temptation was part of our story – and of our commitment.

Before meeting each other, we were in a hurry; work, home, friendships, sexuality, gatherings, ambitions, delusions. We had to do everything in one day. As soon as we met, time slowed down, like a Terrence Malick film; it moved without fluctuation, only uncanny silence, a liberating immobility, the single musical note of paradise where there is no tension or break or mutation.

I look around now. I see glimpses of your shaking hands, now and then. Some shadow, a feeling that someone is moving around me, the crazy idea that you are behind the door, the premonition that you will call me. A verse from a forgotten poet springs up to my lips frequently: *impalpable impressions on the air / a sense of something moving to and fro.* I studied cooking for you, so that you could eat well and recover. Now, I do not cook. I threw out all expensive spices, cheese, meat and pasta. The angelic scents or pepper, nutmeg and cinnamon, the protector saints of our home, have all but vanished. My mother comes to my mind again. After my brother died at fifty, she never cooked again. She was a staunch cook, devoting hours for preparation and making all ingredients "melt together slowly, slowly," as she used to say. But she forgot completely how to cook after he died. "We always make food for others, not for ourselves," she said. I understand what she meant. I have stopped cooking. I don't want to know anything about food.

I went to your grave yesterday again. The eerie silence of the cemetery was interrupted by screechy birds and some handyman's work. I looked around. Your parents are buried there, and your sister. You are all next to each other again. And me, the foreigner, brought you all together, just like in your happy and disturbing days in Woy Woy. I stood alone over the grave, fell onto my knees. "Rob," I said. "Give me a sign, share your world with me." And you responded with the sound of a truck passing by and of kookaburras squawking. "I will stay here," I said, "I will wait for you to speak to me again. I will be buried with you. I will never see the green pine trees of my motherland again, or the blue sea or my native village. I will stay here. With you. My nativity, you. My entombment, you. The ground in the groundless existence of my remaining years." What strange creatures we are, never accepting the unspecified and the irreversible.

But this story is about you and not me, I have said that already, I think. Many people who lose a beloved partner, friend, child or parent write long letters about themselves and what the departed meant to them. They also try to write about the great myths of their mind: God, chance, love, history. This letter is about you and says nothing about me although it reveals everything about us. I don't know who I am anymore, what I have done, how good I was in my profession. What matters is our confluence in time, our convergence, our union. It speaks through them about you – and about us through you.

You didn't have the time to give your agony and creativity a concrete form and a solid structure. You started late and you knew it. Music was in your breathing: you played and taught it with passion and humor. You knew that you didn't have the connections to be accepted by the privileged few who make it to the big orchestras. You were also not competitive enough; you thought that value would be accepted immediately, that others' innate attraction to beauty would be sufficient.

On several occasions you'd recall the precious remark by Winifred Durie, your viola teacher back in '82: "You have the warmest, most velvety sound amongst all those who play the viola today." You kept repeating it. You engraved those remarks in your heart, which is the most authentic home for art. Your insecurity never let you play political games, to embody ruthless aggression or blind ambition. You were dismissed by famous music teachers because of your class rather than a lack of merit. You were an artist not a virtuoso: you didn't show off, you engaged intimately with the sounds. As you played you became the music. "I don't have the killer instinct," you said, "to pursue a career in the music scene of Sydney." And gradually you withdrew and left behind the toils and ambitions of your youth.

After you left, I received a letter from a former student of yours, now a member of the Berlin Philharmonic, and another, from the Boston Philharmonic. Without you, they "would have remained amateurs," they said. "He made us perfectionists," both added. Another message from Tokyo: "He was the mentor who initiated me into deep music," she wrote. I had never heard the concept of deep music before. I knew how important music was to you, especially string music. Then I understood: it was the deep music indeed. The music of the psyche, springing from our desire to be heard, to reproduce the primal sigh of awe and despair that has made art possible since the beginning of human consciousness. Teaching music became the passion of your life: giving your sensitivity and receptivity to young people who responded with passion and inventiveness.

Some people say well-meaning words of consolation: "You will be free now. You can rebuild your life. You must find a hobby." Freedom means surrendering your existence to what you mostly love in this created world of imperfections. Grief generates inertia, an unwillingness to act. But every time I look at our photographs, or watch some videos, I relive your graceful simplicity, as an eternity within this moment, a rupture in the monotony of this emptiness. It transforms my present into diverse instants of grace in nature where the sacred eternally abides.

Meanwhile your flowers have started dying, one after the other. Your secret garden where you could hide and think and silently weep vanishes day by day. I try to look after them, water, prune and feed them but they know something has changed: it is not you but a stranger, someone pretending to look after them; they sense that he is doing it for you and not for them. The azalea wilted first and then the roses and the frangipani, the carnations, the waratah, the kangaroo paws, the cactuses, the small gumtrees, the rosemary, the banksias, the basils, everything. Your colorful small petunias became dry leaves, a brownish mass of dead phantasmagorias. The promise that each flower represented now lies numb and sealed in rotting buds. One green cypress remains, your Spartan, which reminded us of the color around Olympia, and one small olive tree, which you caressed so fondly, our ultimate longing for roots. I look at them and they castigate me. "He left us," they rustle, "now leave us alone, go away. We are looking for Robert's eyes, his touch, his warmth. It's not you." This is what they are saying every time I try to look after them. They ignore me. I feel helpless.

At the heart of every relationship there is a garden. I am doing my best to keep it alive, but the flowers constantly ask about you – and I know not how to explain death to them, loneliness, departure and mourning. "There will be no new spring for us," they say to each other. "We are here to listen to the words of Robert Joseph Meader, calling us to life. He was watering us one by one, patiently and intimately. He was telling us stories. He was our friend. But where is he? It is better never to be born again if he is not here. His hands kept us alive. His voice created our beguiling melancholy." And while I try to explain, they remain distant, ignoring me: I am the stranger now, the alien, the superfluous presence. "Who is he?" they ask each other. "Where is Robert Joseph Meader?" I didn't know that my mind was inhabited by so many pantheistic spirits.

Every sunset I go up into your garden to wish you goodnight. As the sun goes down your face appears like an old icon over the horizon: your green eyes look at me with compassion and your huge smile outlasts my agony. Do not forget me and abandon me in the distractions of daily insignificance. Talk to me when you can and touch me if you are allowed. Together we existed, we explored words together, we pronounced rare adjectives, we imparted our tension to the things that make life livable. I don't want to be myself anymore. I cannot be myself without you. Until the end, I will remain an empty shell without form or substance, driven here and there by chance or inevitability. We didn't grow old together after all. And I don't forgive myself for this. It is not about self-pity; it is about my expulsion to the reign of nothing-ness.

I couldn't sleep last night, and the room was filled with silver birds, cutting through the thickness of my longing. With its azure melancholy the moon lit the corner where I was crouching like a motherless infant. I felt a presence, a gust of wind within the stillness of the stuffy room. "Who are you?" I asked, "you, invisible visitor?" "I am the enigma of loving," a voice said. "I saw you crouching in your bed and wanted to tell you that Robert's green eyes are now in you. Accept them, cherish them, they are in you now, accept them, cherish them. You are nothing without them."

When the voice departed, I opened my eyes and saw you, alive and solid, dressing up for a concert, holding the viola in your hands. "I won't be coming back tonight," you said, "I will sleep with somebody else, do not make food, do not wait for me, I will never come back to our home." I was stunned and horrified. "I don't believe you," I protested. "I believed you for thirty years and now you make me anxious like a confused adolescent, like a child who looks for his father in a crowd, a broken shell on the shores of the Pacific." You opened the door and vanished. The morning birds called me back to reality and when the sun rose, I had to face your luminous absence as an event of life. With my eyes open, I see illusions. With my eyes closed, the full reality of things.

Before the dawn, before the stars were devoured by the sun, I looked at the sky and noticed the Southern Cross for the first time. I have often searched for it, but my eyes, blurred by the velocities of the northern hemisphere, were never able to find it on the firmament. But before the dawn last night it was the only constellation visible on the dark sky, in the cold and nefarious August, three months after you left. "Oh God," I thought, "I am becoming a German romantic, I am looking for stars in the sky at night, I am looking for the souls of the departed in the platonic heaven of beauty recollected."

This is the saddest verse I could send you: only beauty gives meaning to life, spurred on by love. But you are not here, love is gone, so beauty will remain indecipherable, and its yearning, an annoying secret and psychopathic remorse. Solitude looks for origins. We abandon suddenly the warmth of maternal myths and religious domestications. We are taken over by the desire to return to the dominion of the father whom we both despised and longed for. This night I return to my father's home, and I am afraid. I thought that I had outgrown him, and now in your absence, I started looking for his face. You stood at the entrance of the paternal hearth, protective guardian and avenging angel. There is no happiness or rest now, neither light nor joy. Without you, I am a prisoner in my father's home and there is no escape. Together, we gained our innocence, and, now alone, I am punished. Take my hand and guide me away or give me the end I deserve. Deliver my soul to my enemies or absolve me to eternal oblivion.

⌒

Good night my sweet prince and flights of angels carry you to thy rest: life was not always kind to you, but your grace transformed hardships into affection and changed all around you. You brought out the good angels in me, you made me feel that I could be better, that there is an innocent child in me, longing for the opportunity to experience a life not given, the ground to thrive. I was blessed to have been next to you for almost thirty years, the best part of my life. One of my beloved philosophers said: *Ultima hominis felicitas est in contemplatione veritatis.* The greatest happiness of man is found in the contemplation of truth. Now that the contemplation has ceased, where can I find the truth and how can I experience *felicitas*?

Farewell, my sweet prince, I will never forget your gentle face, the sound of your viola, your spirit full of grace under pressure. Now that you are gone, I hope that something of your grace and fortitude will remain in me for the rest of my life. I learned more about life through you than any book or theory. You showed me the intimacy that cleanses the mind from all compulsions and transforms desire into a tender touch at the shores of childhood. Through a single kiss, I absorbed the essence of being and your touch gave me the paradise I longed for when I was baptized in the water and the flame of Jesus.

We write because we are wounded. This is not simply about you and me anymore. Through sadness, grief and solitude we are all reborn. We bring forth the spring of memories or the autumn of echoes. Forgive the arrogance of the living and the fear of all those left behind. I think of the years to come without you, recollect our journeys, your fingers on the viola, your gaze over the rocks and the tribulations of winter days in remote lands. I found you in Iceland, years before we met, in the snowstorm and the ice and the geysers. I met you in Russia, in the long night journey to Vladivostok when I understood the godless horizons of religion. I had a glimpse of you in Chile on the way to the Patagonian deserts, the vast deserts full of sand and poetry. Or in Holland where I searched for meaning and found disillusionment and the ghosts of the father. Even in the small village where I was born: you were there, laughing through the olive trees, the sacred rivers and the epiphanic myths. You were the breeze that animates existence, the legends of my grand-mother, the emotional geometries that shaped me on my way to Damascus.

We are all afraid of wordless infinity, we search for the ultimate prescnt, the full moon of a perpetual August in the land of our childhood fairytales. You gave me the rudder to orient myself towards the Ithaca of a second birth, through music, gesture, and the human gaze, yes, the silent human gaze. There is no will, power, knowledge, imagination: only the impregnable desire to go back home. I am homesick and lost and will resist the sharpness of death through grace or perseverance. You gave my home to me, you awoke me in the clarity of the ocular heart, the heart that sees through the complexities of being and the mysteries of desire. I can face the father now. I can confront him. I am your son, now. I will be pure and nocturnal, a blind insect separated from your luminous eyes.

"There is somebody missing from our table tonight," Kostas our friend said, ninety-two days after you left, when we out for dinner. We talked about the grand themes of Australian culture; weather, sports and television. "There is somebody missing from our table tonight," he repeated. We had some medium rare rump stake, with salad and chips, chicken schnitzel with mushroom sauce and a big hamburger. Somebody was missing from our table that night. I felt it myself. We had beer and lemon squash and red wine. We stayed for two hours, talked with each other, made arrangements. As we were leaving, I looked back, just in case I'd forgotten something, and there you were, on a chair at the next table, devouring a big hamburger with chips and salad. You looked around with affection and distance, you looked at me as if we had never met, smiled and kept eating. Kostas then asked: "Did you notice the man who sat at the table next to ours? Didn't he look like Robert?" As we walked out, I turned my head to have a final glimpse of the man, who smiled at me with your green eyes, Venetian lips, white teeth, your beautiful face. He waved goodbye and, as my eyes blurred, he nodded with understanding. Was it you? Am I going to spent what is left of my life with apparitions and phantoms? Maybe what death does best is open the gates to the dimensions where space and time converge, and the ultimate mingling of essences takes place.

Yesterday, tomorrow, today, all centuries and moments, all happen in one place and all places, childhood, adolescence, adulthood, old age, converge into fleeting and archetypal images, bringing back to us the awe and admiration we felt when we saw our first full moon above the sea while dolphins were dancing over the waters, and the gentle breeze of divinity covered us with mercy, bliss and hope. You showed me the way when I had no direction. You gave me a destiny when I was consumed by trivialities. I know that you would dislike all such praise, but this is a prayer more than anything else. It is idolatry, I know. It is worship of the ephemeral. I pray to the elements, the night, the day, the trees, the sky, the sea, the minerals, the heavy water, the flowers, the grass, the soft light of our birthdays, to all of them together, to their absolute continuum, that begets something beyond all its parts, which some call nature and others god. Yes, I can do no more but worship the ephemeral and, yes, yes, the graven images of my fallibility. Your death emptied me of everything:

I will be hollow and complete when his angel comes for me.

Something else I must tell you: I will never use your loss as a pretext to wallow in my doubts or indulge in my certainties. We both believed that our meeting was the improbable confluence of unrelated events, the ultimate fruition of the accidental. From that random encounter, something new emerged, made from both of us but also greater than us. The accidental became inevitable and imminent. Love was the catalyst. Love galvanized the transformation. I will live exploring its arcane realm until my end.

C.S. Lewis brings up time and again the question of theodicy: where is God when we suffer? Suffering presupposes love, empathy, attraction, call it what you like. And who can tell what truth is proclaimed in the tombs? What love the grave declares? What mercy is glorified in the night of death? None but ourselves can bear our grief or carry away our sorrow: we will keep living wounded, broken, inarticulate, there will be no rest for our soul, no peace for our body, no one will wipe the tears from our eyes. Dust and ashes and fading marks, no Alpha and Omega, only silence beyond words, only void before writing.

The world turned primeval after you left, edgier, unchiseled, uncouth. Suddenly, I became aware of the significance of everyday things, which I once ignored and overlooked. The little trinkets from your childhood, the faded photographs of your adolescence, the few writings of your maturity. And with them, the dignity of small creatures, the dark abysses of flowers, the hidden colors of gloomy twilights, the presentiments of a personal conflagration, the certainty of a silent emptying of all existence into the hard and persistent consciousness of stone, wind, fire and infinity. I now remember how upset you were when your eighteen-year-old cat Debussy vanished, eloping to the dense woods around Woy Woy to die alone. You searched for weeks and after you gave up, you sighed and said: "Another link to the world of my youth is broken."

It happened when your mother had her first stroke, though fortunately you were with her that night and saved her life. For almost ten years, you looked after her, as she moved from one nursing home to another. You visited her every day. The three of us had some great moments together. Christmas and Easter at a nursing home. It sounds depressing and miserable, but it was beautiful and humanizing. "The happiness," you said, "the happiness in the eyes of these aged people, because they haven't been forgotten. Isn't it fascinating?" I still remember with emotion those sorrowful and uplifting hours.

An involuntary snapshot: July 2015, Veronica, Andras, you and I. Blackheath. In front of a red cake. Celebrating the birthday of Veronica's father and mine. Their immense and rapturous garden. Andras, optimism. Veronica, faith. I, nostalgia. You, happiness. I recall, I recall, I recall, like an alchemist struggling to achieve his philosophical stone, while abiding in the oeuvre au noir, the dark blackness of elements without transmutation.

Your absence opened the gates to things I considered lost in the Hades of my unconscious. More and more the image of my ridiculous father resurfaces. I relive his failures, his lack of self-awareness, his utter emptiness. Your absence makes space for such abysmal creatures that destroyed our childhood to emerge and trans-figures them into sinister omens and beatific images. Those Sundays in our youth, full of rage and affection, are now becoming moments of pious restoration. We talked about them many times: so far apart, in different places of this forlorn and magnificent planet, the same magic, the same bitterness, the same confusion.

We were the children of children: of a man and a woman, who didn't live their own childhood.

In the beginning they thought that they could live it through us, but they were soon disappointed, frustrated, angry. And we became the enemy, proof of their inability to be themselves. Expelled from the love of our parents we struggled to achieve our own journey back to our childhood, be kind to those same parents, be content with our birth, be grateful for all. We did it, you and I, we did it. Yes, I am certain we did it. In the end, we relived their childhood, we purified it, we extracted its melody and sadness, and we understood what it was all about.

I don't care about any divine plan and will never appeal to the sparkling whims of coincidence. There is no plan, and no one can plan anything: accident prevails and foreknowledge avails not. In the memories of others, eventually, we all become icons: abstracted, otherworldly, geometric. Soon even this is gone, and we are transferred even further, to the aniconic sphere of being, mere names that existed sometime, about which nothing is known. We look back, through the souls of those who loved us and made our face the abode of their inner being, with compassion and sorrow. One is inextricably linked to the other: our beloved is dead for us to accept death as our own destiny too. Is it possible? I am struggling, Rob, I am struggling. Help me in my incoherence. I cannot even use rhetoric to avoid the problem.

Can we embrace death because our beloved died? Is that dark abyss in any way lovable? I cannot reconcile myself with this horrible darkness. When my mother died, I felt relief. Her suffering ended, dementia stopped hollowing out her beautiful face: she found rest and expiation. She was eighty-seven, the age that her father, mother and sister died. I cried out to all terrible angels and shouted her name to all directions but soon I realized that it was more for the premonition of departing and less about her actual death. I keep a joyful image of her in my mind – almost a funny one.

The last time I saw her, in August 2019, you had just come out of the ordeal with your eye. You felt better so I left you for twenty-four days alone, the longest period we have been away from each other. I had to see her. We knew that that would be our last meeting. One night, she touched my forehead with hers and simply said: Goo-goo-de. I knew what she meant. From the fogginess of her lost sanity, like all earth animals, she smelled that the ship was sinking, that she would have to jump into the ocean to escape. I felt a chill over her skin. "Bye-good, b-goog, bood…" she warbled incoherently. But her message was clear. This is how animals communicate before the eruption of a volcano, a cataclysm, or an earthquake. Like them, she talked in growls, grunts and howls, returning to prehuman certainties before the ambiguities of verbal thinking. She was warning me of the approaching night. "Go and find your father again," that's what she said. "Go back to your father's home. He is expecting you." Strange, so strange. I thought she never loved him. Strange, so strange. I thought I never loved him.

But where is my father's home? And who is my father?

When you first arrived, you released the mystery in all things visible and added shadow to all things invisible. You reconnected me with the forgotten language that my dreams constructed and gave me the images for a story beyond past, present and future. The world hiding in me erupted and gave me forms and myths that rendered presence solid and recognizable. I entered existence because of you. I understood that it is not only me in me. My parents gave me life and you gave me reality. Love desires the real. Through dark forests, endless blue seas, hectic urban architectures, you revealed my silent expectation for our common home. You became the father of my being, the home that was destined for me before I was born, far away on the other side of the planet. "Put your finger in my wounds and you will know who I am". This is the only sentence I remember now from my religion.

There is always an enmity between us and our emotions and only someone else can redeem our life from this imprisonment, from frustration and incommunicability. Love interrupts the continuum of God because it makes us self-sufficient and complete. Plato got it right with his double people in the *Symposium*: it is not sex that holds people together but the quest for completeness. Love answers the only question worth pursuing: "What is it that us human beings really want from each other?" Sometimes, unexpectedly, and unconsciously, love offers us the answer, and we feel restored and recon-structed. The punishment for love is death; this is what is meant when we sing that love is as cruel as death. I know, Rob, I know, you will tell me that there is no after-life, no mystery, no recollection, and we should not have empty hopes. But love subdues us to the dominion of the unseen and the ineffablc.

When death comes, we enter their realm, which others call nothingness. I think I know, my love, it exists but also it doesn't: it is peculiar, paradoxical, like human imagination destined to create forms and images that are not out there but rather in here. Death is our atonement for completing each other: human presence must end, human life must vanish, only bones must remain, chewed out slowly by the seasons, and the hidden dinosaurs of consciousness. Loving unveils our truth about being and knowing: we all become guilty. Death is our atonement for aspiring to regain our wholeness. That's the final affliction to our existence, the last reconciliation with our own ephemerality and the limitations of our mortal frame.

Our confluence made me see my birth again, rekindle my innocence, converse with my beloved dead friends, hold on my palm the force that makes everything jingle and chime. You, my eternal and only purgatory: you have cleansed me from delusional virtues and restored me to my natal purity. We are here to make a home and lose it. Plant a tree and burn it. Say few words and forget them. The great god of our life, oblivion. The angel of deliverance and salvation, oblivion. Our only reason to be here, oblivion. Only our insecure fathers knew how to make permanent homes. We, safe and demanding, erect transient buildings where we squander our precarious privileges. We were the first generation without fathers, doomed to look for the paternal source, while distracted by maternal affections. Your love was my home and now, destitute and banished, I must return to the unknown father and reclaim what was always mine.

You were the remedy against time and thirty years passed so fast. Love crucifies time and makes space for our transfiguration. In inexpressible annihilation, I watched the hidden blood of all things emerge in front of me. The flames of the real envelop my senses, but as with the heroes of old, they leave a single spot vulnerable and fragile. "Find a heart in which to abide," they whisper. "Or else you will be alone now and suffer and feel lost. Robert is not here anymore. He was separated from you, snatched up in the clouds of the unconditional and the infinite."

This is how I console myself, in order to survive each day and ignore the countless omens and apparitions emanating from the arcane structures of our rational consciousness. "Your absence has made me a stranger to myself," I whisper sometimes, without really understanding what I mean. There is a moment in life when the body retracts and gathers itself in premonition. It abandons language and rejects identity. It struggles to find the instinct for survival. It translates itself into the animal language of unconscious existence, lurking for its unsuspicious and guileless prey.

Every day becomes a station towards an absurd and wordless experience. And I am no Buddhist. I do not suffer because I see things as they are. I feel liberated, complete, when I dive into the things themselves. Leukemia is not a gift and I take no delight in death. I don't want to encounter that or be lost in it. Both will happen irresistibly and irrevocably. Nothing is permanent but nothing also is an illusion.

It is the concreteness and the solidity in the people we lose that overwhelms us with grief and anxiety. Life is iconoplastic because we are real. We make images because we are real. We exchange images because we are real. We love images because we are real. Only those who believe in the real can articulate a theology. Someone was here yesterday: occupied this specific space, used these tangible objects, uttered these specific words. And now he is not here and will never be back. We are left with images we constructed about him. I think that I can accept this and suddenly I touch the objccts he liked, use the same words, and share the space he occupied, and everything collapses. Certainties, decisions, plans. "You must move on," some say. "We all eventually die," they add.

"Move forward with yoga!" The whirlwind of absence sweeps everything away. "I wish you were here," I repeat. "Come back. Have as many lovers as you want. Betray me. Ridicule me. Ignore me. But be alive." There is no closure in this process. I cannot learn anything from this. Mourning is alien to my nature. Less than three months after you left, it has grown roots in me, it has become a poisonous weed which destroys my vision, my gaze, the smile that we both cherished so much on our face.

Occasionally, I go to church to be seduced by the timelessness of rituals. If we have no rituals, we are abandoned in a reality without dimensions, qualities, suspended in the degree-zero of being. Our common life was my ritual. Our everyday trivialities connected us to the time beyond clocks and calendars. The chain of sacred movements is broken now; the dance of our gestures frozen. When the proprietor of life will be back, I hope that it will be quick and final. I have prepared my rituals, I have consecrated them, I have lived through them in my mind. When I sense the lethal arrow of the dark archer and see Persephone's smile, I will respond with disdain and contempt because redemption and absolution became real with our time together: without our rituals, life is not worth living. I remember here the verse we loved so much: "The eye is not satisfied with seeing, nor is the ear filled with hearing." We are here to see and not to see; to hear and not to hear. Build our self and get rid of it. Now I am a repetition of myself, a replica of my own being: centerless I fly to distant horizons where I meet my old friends, Sappho, Kochanowski, Novalis, Rilke and Neruda, and stay content. Their images saved me, they saved our time together, the certainty of goodness in all human hearts. You live in all of them, you are their source, my undoing. Without images life is not worth living.

I haven't stopped reading poetry since you left. And suddenly, as I was confronted with your handwriting on a postcard, my mind went back to my youth, when I was eighteen, and the world was fresh and mystical, and a dear friend read for my impressionable sensibility a poem by the French poet Gerard de Nerval. I never forgot the original, as French was always for me the language of melancholy. Its words, rhythms and images generated in me a sorrow that had silently dwelt in my mind ever since. *Je suis le ténébreux, — le veuf, — l'inconsolé, / Le prince d'Aquitaine à la tour abolie : / Ma seule étoile est morte, — et mon luth constellé / Porte le Soleil noir de la Mélancolie.* "I am the dark, the widower, the inconsolable, the prince of Aquitaine, in his ruined tower, my only star is dead, and my constellated lyre is marked by the black sun of melancholy." It was not accident or coincidence. I encountered this poem because I had to experience it. It was a prefiguration of our story. Poems create destinies. We are the unwritten verification of poetic reveries. We are marked by words and rhythms, we carry them within us without even knowing it, for decades, hidden and muted, until one day, the situation that gave them life emerges in us, and the words, ripe, timely and natural, rise triumphant like dark epiphanies or sinister Aphrodites. Death, in a strange way, becomes the disclosure of what connects us with all humans beyond time, from the first cry of the primitive being to the last prophecy of their dreaming mind.

∽

This letter must end. You must be bored by now. You always hated my operatic exaggerations. But being at the end I must go back when all started. That's the only optimism left in me, recollecting the deep image that encapsulates the absolute triumph of grace. Our first meeting, at the Great Hall of Sydney University. Sunday, August 15th, 1993. Your orchestra was playing Carl Orff's *Carmina Burana*. You finished around eight at night. The majestic sandstone room was cold and miserable. While your colleagues celebrated, drank champagne and ate finger food, you were sitting in a corner of the anteroom. I passed through, as a shortcut on the way out. And I saw you: you stood silent, in a niche at the back, partly lit, almost hiding, with your viola in your hands, a detail from an unknown El Greco or Nicolas Poussin. You looked anxious, pale, and romantic, avoiding all noise and commotion. When I looked at you, the magic words sealed in me since my birth jumped up: "That's him, it will be him, no one else but him."

Madness, I know. Folly, I know. Silly youth, I know. I felt that I had seen you before and we had met each other somewhere else. I even knew your name or remembered it vaguely. He must be a Robert, I thought. I approached slowly and said, "Congratulations. It was a subtle performance of such a loud work." You looked at me with curiosity and replied, "Not my cup of tea. But a gig is a gig. What's your name?" "Vras," I replied. "A long Greek name but I've abbreviated for our communications' sake." "Mine is Robert," you replied. My hunch had been right. "You don't mind changing your name?" you added. "I have no serious feelings about names," I replied. "I hope we meet again," you said without both of us making a step away. It was an awkward moment; we wanted to walk apart but couldn't. The electricity was so strong that I found myself moving closer and closer to your personal space. "I must go," I said suddenly, "I will get a cold." "Don't leave me in here," you said almost imploring. "Can we go somewhere for coffee?"

You left your friends, and we walked down to the place that was to become our meeting spot for many months to come. Badde Manors café at the beginning of Glebe Point Road. You told me where you lived, and even indicated certain problems in your life. "I don't want to scare you. I feel unfulfilled with what I am doing," you added evasively. I sensed all these feelings, and I could infer the rest. Suddenly Plotinus' immortal sentence sprang into my mind. Escape of a loner to a loner. I was new in your country, a privileged outsider, an accidental bystander. This is how I wanted to be and knew it would never feel lonely. Only after I laid my eyes on you, I felt how halved I had been all this time. I realised that something had been missing from my life, that you you you had not, until now, been part of my reality. I realised my original sin only after I was exposed to its catharsis. I re-collected your existence from my memory. At that very moment, without thinking, I asked: "Would you like us to grow old together?" You looked at me with astonishment. You tried to look elsewhere. After some seconds of great agitation your turned to me. And you consented. And this is how it started.

"When can we meet again?" I asked. "I will be on a tour around the state with Musica Viva," you replied. "We can meet around the end of September when I will be back." "Why do we have to wait until then?" I gently protested. "What are you doing tomorrow?" "I don't what to jump the queue," you said. "There is no queue," I answered. We arranged to meet at

Dymocks Bookshop in the city the next day. You were thirty or forty minutes late. I was about to leave when you appeared gasping and apologising. This hasn't started well, I thought.

Such meetings went on for some time. We met for coffee, and concerts and movies; we got to know each other's friends, talked about everyday things, our childhoods, our countries. We were both ashamed to talk about our previous love affairs. One night, four months after we met, as we were listening to Rachmaninov's *Vespers*, you leaned your head on my shoulder, closed your eyes, left a soft sigh, and our story began. You didn't say anything sentimental or silly, impertinent, or vulgar. "This choral work needs some strings," you said, and we laughed together. Thirty years later, those moments of grace and redemption form our common biography. This is how we became our own historians and wrote our own story, as human to human, beyond the vicissitudes of our being and the cruel horizons of eternal symbols.

By giving me the centre, you expanded my life to its outermost limits. I will inhabit the rest of my days like a ghost. I will torment my own mind like a demon. I will shadow my own existence like a menace. I will reside in places of wrath, icy places, caves of bitterness and desolation. My lover and friend has been taken away, cut off, put afar in the land of shadows. There is no acquaintance to console or covenant to redeem me. Affliction, bitterness, dust, reproach, my sorrow is my destiny, my body, my existence. No Heidegger can console me, no Plato can make me forget – and Jesus's promises are not enough. Perpetual freefall from now, living the cruel reality in this beloved city of forlornness and abandonment. The fact that I survived your death means that I didn't love you enough. I deserve what happens now: there is no mercy for humans like me, who don't have the strength, or the despair, to love enough beyond themselves.

I have flown to the land of Nod, east of Eden, a place without angels or roads, full of disquietude and trembling, where all freedom, autonomy and beauty are surrendered to somnambulism and necrophany. This is not my land; this is not my home. I don't want to stay in this place. Yet I will be a convict here forever, I will be flying around the great planets of the cosmos like a demented meteorite. I will be an outcast here and until the final moment, this will be my destiny, a sad quest for what I have already found and lost – and I will be happy in my folly and obscurity.

You know, Rob, I am just a shallow and impressionable Mediterranean. I love glittering surfaces, I adore grand exaggerations, I worship the enfleshment of the logos. I don't like dark places; I don't even notice abstractions; I despise all things intangible. I thought of myself as a petulant Greek, and suddenly the abyss of nothingness, the furious energy of all damned souls, gushes out of me, from depths unimaginable, as an offering to a gnostic god who desires our annihilation. Now that the embodied vision is gone, I remain to stir the dust, the ashes and the sand against the soaring winds of forgetting.

People talk to me about you, want to know how I feel, politely ask if there is a way to help. But grief has sent me to exile even from myself. Now it's me who is elsewhere and looks back at his own life with disbelief and anxiety: "Was it really me who experienced all this? Where am I now? What's all this around me" My life is not my life anymore. I had a dream that I was separated from myself and looked at myself from above with compassion and anger: drinking coffee, I shouted at myself, "This is Robert's cup!" Eating, I screamed, "This is Robert's plate!" Sleeping, I hissed at my own ear, "Get up! He is not with you anymore." Grief led to the birth of a second self, which is my new shadow, my old angel, the purity that I gained with you and the impurity that I have to live with now. Last night, Maisie and Milo were licking my face as I was half-asleep. "Robert," I said, "you are always so fresh!"

I opened my eyes and the dogs looked at me with surprise. "We are not Robert," they said. "Or maybe we are?" And I felt sadness, naked sadness, like the young boy in the garden of Gethsemane.

Are we really born in vain? Did you suffer so much in vain? Is dust our only eternity? Has your death been just an administrative error or a penitential sacrifice for past negligence? My time flows and unflows, and it's not my time anymore, but it's made of weak and needy elements, disguising my bondage to nowness, as I watch the news, sitting in your spot in front of the telly. Time resurfaces as the dark knight: your love had suspended it but now it comes back as the nothing the nothing the nothing, which plunders and demolishes and devastates, leaving ruins where our home stood and uneasiness where serenity flourished.

With this farewell, I want to paint the turmoil, the ecstasy, the sorrow, the bliss, the intimacy, the calmness, the equilibrium everything ineffable and unknowable I have felt by simply being next to you, spirited, playful, fulfilled. I struggle to orchestrate in words what is beyond language. This is a redemption hymn, a tearful epistle, my threnody to appease the panic of mortality.

I always remember the sublime words of my beloved saint: *cantare amantis est*. Only the lover sings. I will remain only that: your lover who sings of your absence in all tunes imaginable. Can you hear my song at all? I sing in a foreign language in alien shores uprooted from the ancestral burials of my homeland. Who will deliver me from the wastelands of exile? What clemency, what mercy, what pardon will release me from the mists of this perpetual purgatory? Only your memory, only if you remember me.

I will be sending letters to our usual address frequently.

Do not abandon me on the other side of things.

Do not reject my song. Hold on to our memories.

Do not throw me into the pit of oblivion.

Your Vras.

*My deep gratitude to Katia Ariel for her
meticulous and sensitive editing;
Paula Green for her understanding and
enthusiasm; Deborah McGowan for her
love and support. Finally, to Veronica and
Andras who agreed to publish this long
letter of grief and contrition.*